83494

It's My Party

A Republican's
Messy Love Affair with the GOP

PETER ROBINSON

WARNER BOOKS

A Time Warner Company

Also by Peter Robinson

Snapshots from Hell: The Making of an MBA

Copyright © 2000 by Peter Robinson
All rights reserved.

Warner Books, Inc., 1271 Avenue of the Americas, New York, NY 10020
Visit our Web site at www.twbookmark.com

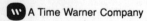 A Time Warner Company

Printed in the United States of America

First Printing: August 2000

10 9 8 7 6 5 4 3 2 1

Library of Congress Cataloging-in-Publication Data

Robinson, Peter, 1957–
     It's my party : a Republican's messy love affair with the GOP / by Peter Robinson.
     p. cm.
     ISBN 0-446-52665-7
     1. Republican Party (U.S. : 1854–) I. Title.

JK2356 .R47 2000
324.2734—dc21   00-028996

For my mother and father

Alice May Booth Robinson
Theodore Herbert Robinson

and my brother

Donald Joseph Robinson

Omnia cooperantur in bonum

CONTENTS

STILL REPUBLICAN AFTER ALL THESE YEARS

I grew up Republican. There were extenuating circumstances.

I was born to Republican parents and raised in a Republican neighborhood. (A big family named Federowicz lived a couple of streets away from us, and I see now that as Polish Catholics they may have been Democrats all along. It is a measure of just how Republican our neighborhood was that all these years later I find the thought of Democrats in our midst unsettling.) Thus I took the Republican imprint before I was old enough to understand what was happening.

Yet it is difficult for me to escape all responsibility here. After attaining the age of reason—or at least the age at which I could legally drive, drink, and vote—I remained a Republican. In college I even became something of a campus politician, editing the opinion page of the college newspaper, writing a political column, and contributing to an upstart conservative newspaper, the now notorious *Dartmouth Review*. Studying at Oxford for a couple of years after graduating, I infuriated my dons by revealing an enthusiasm for Margaret Thatcher—cheering for Tories is what Republicans do when they find themselves in England—and when I returned home I became in effect a professional Republican, taking a job in the Reagan White House.

I was a speechwriter. I name the position because it carried a particular requirement. Broadly speaking, the Reagan administration was divided between pragmatists and true believers. Speechwriters were true believers. Nobody was ever likely to ask a deputy assistant secretary of commerce or labor whether he believed Reagan was right to call the Soviet Union an "evil empire." But the speechwriters? We *had* to believe Reagan was right. We were the ones who had come up with the line. I believed in nearly every word Ronald Reagan uttered. I mean it. When I did disagree with Reagan it was because I thought he was being too soft, not too hard. (The chief of staff, Donald Regan, once told the speechwriters to go easier on Gorbachev. We refused. Regan had to troop us into the Oval Office to hear it from the president himself.)

Even after leaving the White House I continued to take steps that look Republican. First, I went to business school. Now, students at business schools are less Republican than you might think—in a poll of my classmates, Michael Dukakis led George Bush for president—but when they graduate, often walking into the highest tax bracket the same day they walk into their new jobs, they begin migrating to the GOP.* At my class's tenth reunion this past spring, you couldn't have spilled a beer without splashing a Republican. After business school I spent a year working for Rupert Murdoch, then a year working for the chairman of the Securities and Exchange Commission. A media mogul and a capitalist tool—fitting items on a Republican résumé. Finally I joined the think tank where

---

*GOP stands for Grand Old Party. I've looked at every political dictionary I could find to learn where the term originated. Nobody seems to know. It simply begins popping up in newspaper accounts in the late nineteenth century. I happen to like the term—it conveys both warmth and a certain amusement—so I employ it throughout this volume.

I now work. Although it avoids partisan ties, the think tank espouses free market principles, endearing itself, not surprisingly, to members of the GOP. The name of the think tank, I had better admit, is the Hoover Institution. That would be "Hoover" as in "Herbert." Herbert Hoover founded the institution in 1919. Nine years later he was elected to the White House. One year after that the Great Depression struck, transforming Hoover's reputation from that of a business genius and humanitarian into that of a glassy-eyed, hard-hearted . . . Republican.

I recognize that the evidence against me is enough to get me hanged. I can picture my body twisting, with a placard, STAUNCH REPUBLICAN or GOP ZEALOT, pinned to my shirtfront. The odd thing is, the lynching party would be wrong. I'm not a zealot. I'm not even staunch. I've always kept a strict distance between myself and the Republican Party. The distance has existed only in my mind, I grant you. But it has been no less real for that.

I learned early in life to place this distance between myself and the GOP. When I was a boy, each day when my father arrived home from work he would open the *Binghamton Evening Press*. I can't tell you the number of times I saw him shake his head in disapproval as he read about yet another lavish spending project enacted by our governor and fellow Republican, Nelson Rockefeller. In those days the Republican Party so dominated New York that the big political divide ran not between Republicans and Democrats but between Republicans upstate, where we lived, and Republicans in New York City, where Nelson Rockefeller lived, and where we couldn't even imagine living. Republicans upstate were decent and frugal. Republicans in New York City were extravagant, with their own money and that of the taxpayers alike. You might have to share a political party with such people, the look on my father's face suggested, but you didn't have to feel pleased about it.

As I've said, this distance between myself and my fellow Republicans stayed with me. During my high school and college years the leading Republicans ran from the shifty-eyed and criminal (Richard Nixon) to the bland and hapless (Gerald Ford). If the GOP was the minority party, it was easy enough to see why, and I viewed the Republican Party with the same faint disgust that I imagine must characterize sports fans who follow the Chicago Cubs, the Boston Red Sox, and other perennial losers. Later, during the Republican resurgence of the 1980s, I gave my heart to Ronald Reagan, for reasons I will discuss in due course, but never, even then, to the GOP itself. It may seem a small matter, but I feel sure one of the reasons was that I had to tag along with the president or vice president to so many Republican fund-raisers. Fund-raisers were events that rich people put on for the benefit of other rich people. Or so it certainly seemed. At a fund-raiser you could spend as long as you wanted studying the crowd, which would be milling around the ballroom of a hotel or the living room of a huge private home, but the only people of modest means you'd ever spot would be the ones in uniform, tending the bar or circulating with trays of drinks and canapés. I knew the Republican Party championed economic opportunity for the little guy as much as for the plutocrat—I was writing speeches that said so. But at a fund-raiser you could see that for a lot of people belonging to the Republican Party was like belonging to a club. A very good club, judging from the size of the shrimp.

The years since Ronald Reagan left the White House have done nothing to make me feel more at home in the GOP.

George Bush? A likeable man—I came to know him well when I wrote speeches for him. But in some ways he was like those well-heeled Republicans at whom my father used to shake his head. I once heard a member of his staff chastise Bush, then vice president, for wearing striped cloth watchbands. "It looks too preppie," the staffer said. Bush replied, "I like it and I'm keeping it. That's the way I am." Bush was right. If he'd gotten rid of his striped watchbands he'd have been engaging in pure artifice, pretending to be something he wasn't. But the staffer had a point, too. A lot of Americans found it difficult to feel comfortable with a politician from such a patrician background. There were times when I was one of them. Bob Dole? I flipped channels to avoid watching the 1996 GOP convention nominate Dole for president. All those good people, attempting to whip themselves into a state of enthusiasm for a candidate who had no idea why he was running.

Spendthrifts such as Nelson Rockefeller, suspicious characters such as Richard Nixon, bumblers such as Gerald Ford, self-satisfied rich people such as the ones I encountered at fund-raisers, patricians such as George Bush, time-servers such as Bob Dole. There was always so much in the Republican Party of which I disapproved.

"Of *course* there was always a lot of stuff in the GOP of which you disapproved," my friend David Brady recently told me. A professor of political science at Stanford, David is a big man who speaks bluntly. He and I talked over the Republican Party repeatedly while I was writing this book. "The GOP is a political party, for Pete's sake," David said. "It tries to put together the views of tens of millions of Americans. Most people don't even approve of all the people in their own family. How is anybody ever going to approve of all the people in an organization that includes something like

30 percent of all Americans? A distance between yourself and the Republican Party, my backside. You're just looking down on political activists the way everybody does. Let me ask you this. How many times have you ever voted for a Democrat?"

I swallowed hard. The answer was none.

David laughed. "That's good, Peter," he said. "That's a real distance you're keeping there."

My views were Republican, I voted Republican, I had worked in a White House that was Republican. Whatever the distance from the GOP that I may have cultivated in my own mind over the years, it was nothing anybody else would ever have been able to detect. I had to admit it. I was as Republican as they come. That may have been obvious to you as soon as you began reading this introduction, but it came as a rude awakening to me.

The country may be in for a rude awakening of its own.

In the 2000 elections, all three branches of the federal government will be in play as they are only a couple of times in each century. In Congress, both chambers are at stake. In the House, the Republican majority is tenuous. Either party could capture the chamber outright. In the Senate, the GOP appears likely to retain its majority. Yet if the Democrats win enough seats, they could persuade northeastern Republicans to join them in a liberal coalition, effectively bringing the chamber under Democratic control. The White House will have no incumbent running for reelection for the first time since 1988. Either party could win it. The Supreme Court and the federal bench, both almost evenly divided between liberal and conservative judges, could each see its balance tipped by the new president's appointments—and the new president, again, could be a member of either party.

Of course, the GOP could lose all three branches. Losing comes naturally to Republicans. Look at Congress. From 1954 to 1994 the Republican Party failed to achieve a single majority in the House of Representatives while eking out majorities in the Senate in only eight years out of forty. Or look at the White House. After Republicans had held the White House for twenty-eight of the forty years from 1952 to 1992, political scientists had come to refer to the GOP as the "presidential party." Then George Bush found a way to lose to Bill Clinton. Bush's margin of defeat was six percentage points, which in presidential politics isn't even close. Four years later the Republican Party turned down a number of attractive candidates for president to nominate Bob Dole instead. Dole's margin of defeat was eight percentage points. If the GOP loses in 2000, count on a lot of gracious concession speeches. Republicans have had practice.

Yet the scenario for a GOP victory isn't all that implausible. It goes like this. The Republican Party nominates an appealing presidential candidate, perhaps, to name the leading contender as I write, George W. Bush, the governor of Texas.* In winning the White House, Bush pulls fifteen or twenty new Republicans into the House of Representatives, securing a small but solid Republican majority. In the Senate, most of the nineteen Republicans up for reelection are returned to office, while seats the GOP loses are offset by seats, possibly in Virginia and Nevada, that the GOP picks up. With Republicans in control of the Senate, which of course will have to confirm his appointments, President George W. Bush will proceed to fill the vacancies that arise

---

*My publisher is squeezing the schedule as much as possible, but I'm still having to compose these words almost six months before the book will appear.

on the Supreme Court and the federal bench just as he pleases.

A Republican sweep. The thought takes some getting used to, like Einstein's negative curvature of the universe.

The last time the GOP held all three branches of the federal government was some seven decades ago. (In the elections of 1930, the GOP majority in the House of Representatives was reduced to just two seats and Republican deaths soon gave the chamber to the Democrats. Then, in the elections of 1932, the GOP lost to the Democrats in a landslide, seeing the Democrats capture majorities in the House and Senate alike while the Democrat Franklin Roosevelt tossed the Republican Herbert Hoover out of the White House.) The population of the United States seven decades ago was only 120 million, our navy was no more powerful than that of Great Britain, and we were in a Great Depression that would throw one laborer in four out of work. Today the population of the United States is 274 million, our military might is greater than that of all other nations combined, and we are creating a new information economy that is transforming the globe. If the GOP wins in 2000, it will take command of the most formidable nation in history.

Yet this represents a moment of unusual uncertainty for the GOP. It no longer has a leader of the stature of Ronald Reagan. It finds itself divided between social conservatives, who place morality at the center of their politics, and economic conservatives, who favor low taxes and limited government but take a laissez-faire view of social issues. Although in the 1998 elections the GOP did well in most of the country, in California, home to one American in ten, the GOP suffered an enormous blow, watching its senatorial candidate lose by eleven points, its gubernatorial candidate by twenty.

Who will lead the GOP? How will it unify its wings? Can it recapture California? If it wins power in 2000, what will it do with it?

This seemed an opportune moment, in short, to pose a question about my fellow Republicans: Who *are* these people?

To complete this book in time for the 2000 elections, I had to hurry. I read a dozen reference works, made a couple of hundred telephone calls, then began jumping on airplanes to crisscross the country. As I did so I kept a journal, recording what I saw and heard. The result is neither a work of political science nor of history. Strictly speaking it isn't even a work of journalism—I know plenty of journalists who have interviewed far more Republican activists and officeholders than I did. Or than I cared to. My ideal reader is somebody like me, with a family to raise and mortgage payments to make. He has no desire to master the minutiae of the Republican Party, just a sense that he'd like to look into it a little. I wanted to offer him a slender volume, not a tome.

This is instead a travel book, one tourist's notes as he journeyed across the territory of the Republican Party. I interviewed Republicans north, south, east, and west. I examined Republican history and ideology. Throughout my journey I modeled myself on the amateur explorers of the nineteenth century, those avid gentlemen who tried to discover the source of the Nile or locate the tombs of the pharaohs. Like them, I gathered as many facts as I could while keeping an eye out for local color. Like them, I did nothing dozens of others couldn't have done just as well. It's just that I was eccentric enough to do it.

Chapter One

MOUNT REAGAN

Journal entry:

Last night during the taping of a Fox television program, The Real Reagan, *the host, Tony Snow, asked each member of the panel to sum up Reagan's place in history. I found myself launching into a little peroration. "Ronald Reagan's beliefs were as simple, unchanging, and American as the flat plain of the Midwest where he grew up. He placed his faith in a loving God, in the goodness of the country, and in the wisdom of the people. He applied those beliefs to the great challenges of his day. In doing so he became the largest and most magnificent American of the second half of the twentieth century."*

If any of my friends see the program, I suppose they'll take it for granted that I was overstating the case for public consumption—they've certainly never heard me talk that way over lunch on the Stanford campus or at dinner parties in Palo Alto, where we always lace our conversation with a knowing dose of cynicism.

The odd thing is, I meant every word.

In AD 578, the monk John Moschos left the desert monastery of St. Theodosius, set upon a hill or low mount near Bethlehem, to travel the Byzantine world. Inside the monastery, every aspect of existence seemed straightforward for John

Moschos, his beliefs enshrined in the teachings of the church, his life ordered by the monastic disciplines of work and prayer. The moment he left the monastery, he stepped into confusion. The Byzantine empire through which he journeyed was under assault, from the west by Slavs, Goths, and Lombards, from the east by Persians. The cities he toured proved raucous, gaudy, decadent. Even when he visited monasteries he often encountered evidence of strife, on occasion reaching an abbey where he intended to spend the night only to find that it had been burned, its inhabitants marched off to slave markets. In his writings, John Moschos records the teachings of the desert fathers, his intention when he set out. But he also presents long passages in which, amazed and perplexed, he describes his travels, as if unable to believe his eyes unless he set it all down.

I know how the poor monk felt. Just as John Moschos had a place, his desert monastery, that made life seem straightforward, I had a person, Ronald Reagan, who made the Republican Party seem straightforward. I admired Reagan when I was in college and graduate school, then I spent six years working in his White House, devoting a year and a half to writing speeches for Vice President Bush, then four and a half years to writing speeches for President Reagan himself. While Ronald Reagan led the Republican Party, all the important questions for the GOP appeared settled to me. I knew who was in charge. I knew where the GOP stood on every issue. Just as John Moschos, confused on a point of doctrine, needed only to consult his abbot, I, wondering about a point of Republican philosophy, needed only to consult Ronald Reagan's old speeches, radio talks, and newspaper columns. Today nothing about the GOP appears settled to me, and if you are to understand why in the following pages I, like the monk, often sound amazed and perplexed, you will need to take into account my point of departure. John Moschos began on a mount near Bethlehem. I began, if you will, on Mount Reagan.

Probably the best way for me to tell you about Ronald Reagan is to describe the events leading to his 1987 Berlin Wall address.

You may be familiar with the address. The president stood on a blue platform directly in front of the Berlin Wall. In recent months, the president explained, we had been hearing a great deal from the Soviet Union about a new policy of glasnost or openness. If General Secretary Gorbachev was serious about his new policy, the president said, he could prove it. The president set his jaw, then spoke with controlled but genuine anger—not long before, he had learned that a crowd had gathered in East Berlin to hear him, then been forcibly dispersed by the East German police. The last four words of his challenge, each just one syllable, sounded like blows. "Mr. Gorbachev, tear down this wall!"

In May 1987, when I was assigned to write the speech, the celebrations for the 750th anniversary of the founding of Berlin were already under way. Queen Elizabeth had visited the city. Mikhail Gorbachev was due in a matter of days. Although the president hadn't been planning to visit Berlin, he was going to be in Europe in early June, first visiting Rome, then spending several days in Venice attending an economic summit. At the request of the West German government, the president's schedule was adjusted to permit him to stop in Berlin for a few hours on his way back to the United States from Italy. I was told that the president would be speaking in front of the Berlin Wall, that he was expected to draw an audience of around ten thousand, and that given the setting, he probably ought to talk about foreign policy.

I spent a day and a half in Berlin with the White House advance team—the logistical experts, Secret Service agents, and press officials who always went to the site of a presidential visit to make arrangements. All that I myself had to do in Berlin was find material. When I met John Kornblum, the ranking American diplomat in Berlin, I assumed that he would give me some.

John Kornblum had an anxious, distracted air. A stocky man with thick glasses, he kept glancing at the door while he was speaking with me, as if hoping for someone more important to walk in. Kornblum gave me quite specific instructions. Almost all of it was in the negative. He was full of ideas about what the president *shouldn't* say.

West Berlin, Kornblum explained, was the most left-leaning of all West German cities. Its citizens were sophisticated. Reagan should avoid looking like a cowboy. He shouldn't bash the Soviets. He certainly shouldn't mention the Berlin Wall, because the people of Berlin had long ago gotten used to it.

Kornblum offered only a couple of positive suggestions. Reagan should mention American efforts to obtain more air routes into West Berlin. He should play up American support for West Berlin's bid to host the Olympics.

After I left Kornblum, several members of our party were given a flight over the city in a U.S. Air Force helicopter. I'm told that in Berlin these days it is all but impossible to imagine the wall ever existed. I cannot imagine Berlin without it. From the air, the wall seemed less to cut one city in two than to separate two different modes of existence. On one side of the wall lay movement, color, modern architecture, crowded sidewalks, traffic. On the other side, all was drab. Buildings still exhibited pockmarks from shelling during the war. There were few cars. Pedestrians were badly dressed. When we hovered over Spandau Prison, a rambling brick structure in which Rudolf Hess was still being detained, soldiers at East German guard posts peered up at us through binoculars, rifles over their shoulders. The wall itself, which from West Berlin had seemed a simple concrete structure, was instead revealed from the air to be an intricate complex, the East Berlin side lined with dog runs and row upon row of barbed wire.

That evening, I broke away from the advance team to join a dozen Berliners for dinner. Our hosts were Dieter and Ingeborg Elz, who had retired to their hometown of Berlin after Dieter completed his career at the World Bank in Washington. Although we had never met, we had friends in common, and the Elzes had offered to put on this dinner party to give me a feel for their city. They had invited Berliners of different walks of life and political outlooks—businessmen, academics, students, homemakers.

We chatted for a while about German wine and the cost of Berlin housing. Then I related what Kornblum had told me. "Is it true?" I asked. "Have you gotten used to the wall?"

There was a silence. The Elzes and their guests glanced at each other uneasily. I thought I had proven myself just the sort of brash, tactless American that John Kornblum was afraid the president might seem. Then one man raised an arm and pointed. "My sister lives twenty miles in that direction. I haven't seen her in more than two decades. Do you think I can get used to that?" Another man spoke. Each morning on his way to work, he explained, he walked past a guard tower. Each morning, the same soldier gazed down at him through binoculars. "The soldier speaks the same language. He shares the same history. But one of us is a zookeeper and the other is an animal, and I am never certain which is which."

Our hostess broke in. A gracious woman, she had suddenly grown angry. Her face was red. She made a fist with one hand and pounded it into the palm of the other. "If this man Gorbachev is serious with his talk of glasnost and *perestroika,* he can prove it. He can get rid of this wall."

Back at the White House I adapted my hostess's comment, making it the central passage of the speech I drafted. A week later, the speechwriters met the president in the Oval Office. My speech was the last one we discussed. Tom Griscom, the director of communications, asked the president for his comments on my draft. The president simply replied that he liked it. Griscom nodded to me.

"Mr. President," I said, "I learned in Germany that your speech will be heard not only in West Berlin but throughout East Germany." Depending on weather conditions, I explained, radios might be able to pick the speech up as far east as Moscow itself. "Is there anything you'd like to say to people on the *other* side of the Berlin Wall?"

The president cocked his head and thought. "Well," he replied, "there's that passage about tearing down the wall. That wall has to come down. That's what I'd like to say to them."

With three weeks to go before it was delivered, the speech was circulated to the State Department and the National Security Council. Both attempted to squelch it. Rozanne Ridgeway, the assistant secretary of state for Eastern European affairs, challenged the speech by telephone. Peter Rodman of the National Security Council protested the speech in memoranda. Weighing in from Berlin, John Kornblum objected to the speech by fax. The speech was naïve. It would raise false hopes. It was clumsy. It was needlessly provocative. State and the NSC submitted their own alternate drafts—as I recall, there were no fewer than seven, one written by Kornblum himself. In each, the call to tear down the wall was absent.

The week before the president left for Europe, Tom Griscom began summoning me into his office each time State or the NSC came up with a new objection. Each time, Griscom had me tell him why I believed State and the NSC were wrong and the speech, as I had written it, was right. (Once I found Colin Powell, then national security adviser, in Griscom's office waiting for me. I was a thirty-year-old who had never held a job outside speechwriting. Powell was a decorated general. We went at it nose-to-nose.) Griscom was evidently waiting for an objection he thought Ronald Reagan himself would find compelling. He never heard one.

In Venice the day before the speech was to be given, the deputy chief of staff, Ken Duberstein, decided that the objections from State and the NSC had become so strident that he had to present them to the president himself. When he finished briefing the president, Duberstein tells me, an exchange along the following lines took place.

REAGAN: (A twinkle in his eye) I'm the president, aren't I?
DUBERSTEIN: Yes, sir, Mr. President. We're clear about that.
REAGAN: So I get to decide whether the line about tearing down the wall stays in?
DUBERSTEIN: That's right, sir. It's your decision.
REAGAN: Then it stays in.

As *Air Force One* left Venice for Berlin the next morning, the fax machines on board began to whir. Making a final effort to squelch the speech, State and NSC were submitting yet another alternate draft. Tom Griscom never even took the fax to the forward cabin.

The reasons I gave my heart to Ronald Reagan are all right there. The boldness. The clarity of vision. No one else would have given that speech—certainly not George Bush. I liked Bush, as I have said, but I had worked with him long enough to know that his first reaction on seeing my draft would have been to ask, "What's State say about this?" Reagan didn't care what State said. He cared about tearing down the wall.

There is a school of thought that Ronald Reagan managed to look good only because he had clever writers putting words in his mouth. But Jimmy Carter, Walter Mondale, Bob Dole, and Bill Clinton all had clever writers. Why was there only one Great Communicator? Because Ronald Reagan's writers were never attempting to fabricate an image, just to produce work that measured up to the standard Reagan himself had already established. His policies were plain. He had been articulating them for decades—until he became president he wrote most of his material himself. When I heard Frau Elz say that Gorbachev should get rid of the wall, I knew instantly that the president would have responded to her remark. And when the State Department and National Security Council tried to block my draft by submitting alternate drafts, they weakened their own case. Their drafts were drab. They were bureaucratic. They lacked conviction. They had not stolen, as I had, from Frau Elz—and from Ronald Reagan.

In my judgment, Ronald Reagan was the greatest president of the last five decades and one of the half dozen greatest in our history. When he gave the Soviet Union a few good kicks, causing it to fall in on itself, he drew the Cold War to a peaceful end. When he enacted his economic program, he set in place the conditions that have led to eighteen years of almost uninterrupted economic growth. When he spoke of his beliefs—in God, in the goodness of the nation, in the wisdom of the people—he changed the very spirit and temper of the country, replacing the bitterness of Vietnam and Watergate with a buoyant, self-confident patriotism.

The worst that can be said against Reagan is that he allowed federal deficits to pile up. Although often repeated, the allegation is silly. Democrats controlled the House of Representatives during all eight years of the Reagan administration, making it impossible for Reagan to cut domestic spending as much as he wanted. Yet while Reagan's economic program added $1.4 trillion to the federal debt, it added $17 trillion to American asset values—the market value of land, stocks, houses, patents, and all other assets in the United States rose from $16 trillion in 1981 to $33 trillion in 1989—providing a return of twelve to one.

Today the federal budget is no longer in deficit but in surplus. Why? For two reasons. The economy continues to boom—thanks to Ronald Reagan. And we have been able to scale back our military, saving tens of billions each year, because the Cold War is over—thanks to Ronald Reagan. President Clinton may take all the bows he wishes, but his principal contribution to the surplus was to stay out of the way as the budgetary implications of Reagan's policies worked themselves out.

Reagan accomplished all that he did without ever losing his sense of proportion about life itself. He remained sane. I witnessed a particularly telling instance of Reagan's normalcy just a few months after he left office.

In Los Angeles for a couple of days in the spring of 1989,

I stopped by the suite of offices that had been set up for former President Reagan and his staff. As he stood to greet me, Reagan had the same twinkle and shine in his eyes and the same knowing nod that he had possessed during eight years in the White House. "Just doing a little writing," he said, gesturing to a pad of paper on his desk. "Now that I'm out of office, I have time to get back to writing my speeches myself."

After a moment of small talk, the former president frowned and asked if I had seen the morning newspaper. I had, noticing over breakfast that the *Los Angeles Times* referred to Reagan in two front-page stories. "Saw Risk of Reagan Impeachment, Meese Says," one headline read, while the other stated, " 'Star Wars' Was Oversold, Cheney Says."

"I just don't understand it," Reagan said.

"Neither do I, Mr. President."

"How can a *judge* decide the outcome of a sporting event?"

It took me a moment to realize Reagan was not talking about his administration. He was commenting on the America's Cup. A judge in New York had just awarded the cup to the boat from New Zealand, even though the American boat had put in a faster time. "San Diego Loses America's Cup," the headline stated. "Conner's Use of Catamaran Ruled to be Violation of Governing Deed."

"Well," the former president said, the twinkle returning to his eye, "at least it wasn't a judge *I* appointed."

When I left, I was disappointed at first that the former president hadn't even mentioned world events, let alone imparted any secrets or insights of historical moment. I had had my moment with the man who won the Cold War, and all I had managed to come away with was some talk about a boat race. How could Reagan have done that to me?

But by the time I was back in traffic on the Santa Monica Freeway, I recognized that the former president had given me a very good example of the wisdom and simplicity of spirit that I had always cherished in him. For eight years he had been the most powerful man in the world. Then he set it all down and went back to being as ordinary an American as a former president can be. When Reagan looked at the newspaper, he read about sports.

Pity John Moschos. After his monastery, the world seemed so confusing. Pity me. Ronald Reagan won the Cold War, turned the economy around, and set an example of sanity that makes Republicans today seem ridden with angst. As I set out to learn what the Republican Party now stands for, I scarcely knew where to turn.

Chapter Two

ALONG THE RIPPLING SUSQUEHANNA

Journal entry:

Cast my mind back over the history of the Republican Party, and what do I see? Images of Republican conventions—confetti flying, balloons drifting toward the ceiling, and delegates, festooned with campaign buttons, straw hats perched atop their heads, waving placards as they parade around the floors of huge convention halls to demonstrate for their favorite presidential candidates. I can picture perhaps half a dozen conventions, no more. I see them first in color, gaudy, red-white-and-blue spectacles nominating Bob Dole in 1996, George Bush in 1988 and 1992, and Ronald Reagan in 1980 and 1984. Then the conventions change to black-and-white—my father held on to our old Zenith long after everybody else in the neighborhood had bought a color set. In black-and-white I can go back as far as 1964, calling to mind grainy images of the liberal sophisticate, Nelson Rockefeller, being booed as he attempted to address the convention, which rejected Rockefeller to nominate the rough-hewn conservative, Barry Goldwater, instead. Before that? The conventions begin to flicker, shifting from our family television set to newsreels that I must have been forced to sit through in a high school history class. Dimly,

I can see Thomas Dewey at the convention of 1948 and Alf Landon at the convention of 1936. Then the conventions fade to black.

Nineteen thirty-six. I can get back that far and no farther. Yet the Republican Party was founded in 1854, more than 80 years earlier. Some Republican I am.

I began my journey by turning to the past. Perhaps, I reasoned, I could find the meaning of the present-day Republican Party by reaching back across the decades, beyond Ronald Reagan, to the very founding of the GOP. Disappearing into the library for a couple of weeks—as my journal records, I realized at once that I had some remedial work to do—I discovered bad news. To understand the history of the GOP you have to learn a little bit about the Whigs—yes, the Whigs—and to learn about the Whigs you have to acquaint yourself with the Federalists and the Democratic-Republicans. Even in an account as brief as this one, there is no way to go about it but to begin at the beginning.

How did we end up with a two-party system in the first place?

THE BLUES AND THE GREENS

When they drafted the Constitution, the founding fathers left out political parties, making no provision for them whatsoever. The oversight was intentional. The founders detested parties. James Madison devoted an entire tract, *Federalist Number Ten*, to denouncing parties, or, to use the eighteenth-century term, "factions." "The violence of faction," Madison wrote, leads to "instability, injustice, and confusion." Yet before the nation was a decade old, nearly all the founding fathers, including Madison himself, had gone right ahead and formed themselves into two political parties, the Federalists and the Democratic-Republicans. Why? They had left themselves no choice.

Drafting the Constitution, the founders had been intent on preventing the formation of a powerful central government in the United States like the one that ruled Britain. So they had fragmented power, dividing the government of the new republic into three branches, the executive, the legislative, and the judicial, and encumbering each branch with onerous checks and balances. Then, after the Constitution was ratified and the members of the new government assembled in New York City, the nation's first capital, the founders discovered a problem. It proved difficult to get anything done. To enact a program, the president had to win support for his measures in Congress. To pass a law, Congress had to persuade the president to sign it. To stay on the good side of the Supreme Court, the president and Congress had to coordinate their activities, avoiding measures the Supreme Court might deem unconstitutional.

Imagine for example that you're Alexander Hamilton. Hamilton, President Washington's secretary of the treasury, was determined to build a strong, activist federal government—not as powerful as the government in Britain, but powerful enough to dominate the state governments while directing the national economy. As Hamilton, you suppose yourself to be sitting pretty. This is understandable. You, more than anyone, have the ear of President Washington, and President Washington, more than anyone, holds power. Then you make an ugly finding. Hobbled by the checks and balances the Constitution has placed on his office, even President Washington can accomplish almost nothing on his own. You realize that you need allies—not just a collection of cronies but a formal organization of like-minded men, capable of raising money, recruiting candidates for office, and swaying public opinion. So you get together with Vice President John Adams, and a couple of dozen members of the House and Senate, to form a party, the Federalist Party. Then you obtain backing from your rich friends, bankers in New York and merchants in Boston, and go national, setting up party organizations in all thirteen states. Now you've got something. Now you stand a chance of getting at least some of your program enacted.

Next imagine that you're Alexander Hamilton's foe, Thomas Jefferson. Jefferson, President Washington's secretary of the treasury, wanted to bolster the power of the state governments, not the federal government, and he championed small landholders, distrusting bankers and merchants. When you see the Federalists start to organize, you realize that you have no choice but to organize a party of your own. So you get together with James Madison, a leading figure in the House of Representatives, to found the Democratic-Republican Party. Then you get backing from your own friends, southern planters, and set up your own party organizations in all thirteen states.

Thus the provenance of American political parties. The founders invented them to get out of a jam.

Which brings us to the next question. What's so special about the number two? If Hamilton and Jefferson gave us two parties, why didn't Monroe give us a third? And Madison a fourth? For that matter, why didn't each of the founders establish a party of his own, giving us a couple of dozen? We return, once again, to our fundamental institutions of government. A couple of institutions in particular endow the number two with special properties. The first is plurality elections.

In discussing electoral systems, there is always a danger of getting lost in the jargon of political science—when I was reading about the subject I got lost in the jargon myself. But the point to grasp about plurality elections is simple. Probably the easiest way to see it is to compare plurality elections with majority elections. In majority elections, the winning candidates must capture more than 50 percent—that is, a majority—of the vote. If, in any given contest, many candidates compete, splitting the vote so many ways that none receives a majority, runoff elections are held, pitting fewer and fewer candidates against each other until one finally succeeds. In plurality elections, all that the winning candidates have to do is capture more votes than any of their opponents—that is, a plurality. Runoff elections never occur. Now here is the point. Under a majority system, the candidates who are defeated in each round can throw their support to other candidates in successive rounds, helping the candidates whose views are closest to their own. But under a plurality system, all that minor or doubtful candidates can do is hurt their own causes, drawing votes away from other candidates. Consider, for example, a race in which several liberal candidates compete against just a single conservative. While the conservative keeps the conservative vote to himself, the liberals will split the liberal vote, handing the conservative an easy victory. (As long as I was presenting a hypothetical example, I thought I might as well make it to my liking.) The liberals would do a lot better to get together beforehand, uniting behind a single liberal candidate. Thus in a plurality system it makes sense to have only two candidates in each race. And since it makes sense to have only two candidates in each race, it makes sense to have only two parties.

Third parties do indeed appear. But most remain tiny, like the Libertarian or Green parties. The few that do grow large seldom last. Whenever a third party begins to attract a sizable following, it also attracts the attention of the two major parties, who suddenly find themselves scrambling to discern the source of the third party's appeal. Once they do so, they adjust their own positions accordingly, putting the third party out of business. Just look at the Reform Party. Ross Perot's major issue when he ran for president on the Reform Party ticket in 1992 was the federal deficit. Then the Republican and Democratic parties picked up the issue, claiming to be as dedicated to reducing the deficit as was the Reform Party itself. When Perot ran for president on the Reform Party ticket a second time in 1996, his vote fell from the 19 percent that he had garnered four years earlier to just 6 percent. Now that the federal deficit has been replaced with a federal surplus, the Reform Party must identify an entirely new issue—at this writing Pat Buchanan, seeking the Reform Party's nomination, appears to be running on protectionism, an issue with little national appeal, while Donald Trump, also seeking the Reform Party's nomination, appears to be offering the country only his ego—or remain marginal. In the words of the historian Richard Hofstadter, "Third parties are like bees: Once they have stung, they die."

The second institution that endows the number two with special magic is the presidency. The founders gave us a system of government in which a single prize, the office of chief executive, dwarfs the rest.

In theory at least, many local two-party systems instead

of one national two-party system might have emerged during the early days of the republic. Virginia might have had two parties, Massachusetts two completely different parties, Rhode Island two parties of its own, and so on. A few local parties did originally exist. Yet voting patterns converged on the Federalist and Democratic-Republican parties so quickly that by 1796, when the Federalist John Adams defeated the Democratic-Republican Thomas Jefferson for president, the Federalists and Democratic-Republicans had already become the dominant parties throughout the country. Why?

Lying outside the national two-party system, local parties faced a choice. Either they signed on with one of the two major parties and got the chance to participate in presidential politics, which was the big game even then, or they remained independent and had to observe presidential politics as outsiders. They signed on.

Fragmented power, plurality elections, and presidential politics. Look in the history books, and those are the explanations for the two-party system that you'll find. Yet as I worked in the library, another explanation kept coming to me: human nature itself. I found my mind occupied by the Blues and the Greens.

The Blues and the Greens were political parties in ancient Constantinople. As far as historians can tell they first took shape as groups of sports fans—two of the colors under which chariot teams raced at the Hippodrome were blue and green. The Blues and the Greens each marched through the city, staging demonstrations. They rioted in each other's neighborhoods. They defended their own sections of the city walls when Constantinople fell under attack. From time to time one party or the other even proclaimed an emperor.

What did the two parties stand for? Did the Blues want lower taxes? Did the Greens support more social spending? Did one accuse the other of being soft on the Turks? Who knows? All we can see as we peer back across the centuries is the two parties themselves. And the Blues and the Greens represent just one of dozens of instances throughout history in which people have grouped themselves into two opposing parties. The Blues and the Greens in ancient Constantinople. The Guelphs and the Ghibellines in medieval Italy. The Roundheads and the Cavaliers in seventeenth-century England. The Federalists and the Democratic-Republicans in eighteenth-century America.

Partisanship. The very word suggests shallow-mindedness. Yet partisanship runs deep.

VERSIONS ONE AND TWO

Journal entry:
Reading about the founding of the Republican Party today, I thought back to the plaster bust of Abraham Lincoln that my father kept out in the garage. The bust was too ugly to go inside the house, but my father was too much of a Republican to throw it out.

The GOP, the party of Lincoln. And then again, I've learned, it isn't.

Ignorant as I was, I was prepared to learn a lot when I looked into the GOP's origins. I was unprepared to learn that there are two completely different versions of the way the GOP came into existence.

Version One: In 1854 the Republican Party emerged *ex nihilo,* out of nothing, a popular movement of ordinary Americans in the upper Midwest, far from the centers of wealth, power, or sophistication. The GOP amounted to a spontaneous moral crusade with a single, noble purpose: cleansing the nation of slavery.

Version Two: When it appeared in 1854, the Republican Party drew much of its support from the same regions, economic classes, and ethnic and religious groupings as had two parties that preceded it, the Federalists and the Whigs. The name of the party may have been new. The party itself was old.

Strange though it seems both versions are true. Both inform the Republican Party to this day.

Version One took place against a background of seventy years of compromises between the North and the South over slavery. The first compromise was the Constitution itself, ratified in 1788. To placate the South, the Constitution stipulated that in determining the population of each state—an important exercise, since it was on the basis of its population that a state would be allotted members in the House of Representatives—slaves would be counted right along with white people. (Each slave would count for only three-fifths of a white person. But to the South three-fifths was better than nothing.) To placate the North, the Constitution stipulated that while the import of slaves would remain legal until the end of 1807, as of that date Congress would have the right to bring the slave trade from Africa to an end. (Congress did just that as soon as the stated interval had elapsed.) The next compromise, the Missouri Compromise, took place in 1820. It brought Missouri into the Union as a slave state. But it also brought in Maine, which until then had been part of Massachusetts, as a state in its own right, preserving a balance between the North and South at twelve states apiece. Thirty years later came the Compromise of 1850. It permitted California into the Union as a free state. But it made a number of concessions to the South, including rigorous provisions for the return of runaway slaves and the settlement of a border dispute between New Mexico, a free state, and Texas, a slave state, under which Texas received $10 million in compensation from the federal government.

While these compromises were taking place, the North was prospering, its economy expanding, its men of affairs growing rich on manufacturing, banking, and shipping. About the same as that of the South when the Constitution was ratified, the population of the North grew so much more quickly that by 1820 it was almost 20 percent larger than that of the South, by 1850 almost 60 percent larger. The very prosperity of the North seemed a condemnation of slavery—look, the North said in effect, at all that we have achieved without it. Why should we go on making one compromise with the South after another?

The final compromise, the Kansas-Nebraska Act, took place in 1854.

The act arose from the ambitions of Stephen A. Douglas, the Democratic senator from Illinois, who wanted to be president. Douglas believed that by opening the territory west of the Missouri to settlement he could ingratiate himself with western farmers, who would move into the territory, and with moneyed interests in the East, who would build railroads across it. Yet Douglas faced a dilemma. If he brought Kansas and Nebraska into the union as free states he would infuriate the South. Yet if he brought them in as slave states he would anger the very farmers and bankers whose support he wanted to win. Douglas's solution? To sidestep the issue. The new legislatures of Kansas and Nebraska, he proposed, would decide the question of slavery for themselves. Even before Douglas's fellow Democrat, President Franklin Pierce, signed the act into law on May 30, 1854, northerners and southerners, both eager to claim the two new states for their own sides, began pouring into Kansas and Nebraska. Almost immediately, fighting between the northerners and southerners broke out.

The nation erupted. In the North, the region that concerns us here, patience with the seven decades of compromises over slavery finally snapped. Preachers denounced the Kansas-Nebraska Act in every pulpit from Maine to Illinois. Torchlight parades were held. Newspapers coupled lurid accounts of the fighting in Kansas and Nebraska with diatribes against the South.

In May 1854 a mass outdoors meeting took place in Ripon, Wisconsin, to found a new, anti-slavery party. Two months later, in July, the new party held a convention in Jackson, Michigan, at which it formally adopted a name, calling itself "Republican." The new party grew at an astonishing rate. Within months it had replaced the Whig Party as one of the two major parties in the country. Within two years it had elected a speaker of the house. Within six years it had placed Abraham Lincoln in the White House.

There is only one way to make sense of the speed with which the Republican Party rose to power. You have to see the GOP as a crusade. At the very moment when millions of northerners were suddenly looking for a way to express their outrage, the GOP represented a vehicle for moral protest. Indeed, until the civil rights protests of more than a century later, the Republican Party remained the biggest protest movement the United States had ever seen.

Version Two is nearly the opposite of Version One. While Version One stresses the suddenness with which the GOP emerged, Version Two argues that by the time of the Kansas-Nebraska Act the GOP had already been around for decades.

To grasp Version Two, you have to ask yourself just what kinds of people would have joined a moral movement like the movement in Version One. It certainly wouldn't have been southerners. They saw the Republican movement as an assault on their very way of life. But it wouldn't have been every northerner, either. Laborers in New York, Boston, Philadelphia, and other northern cities had no desire to free the slaves. The very idea unnerved them. When they pictured freed slaves, they pictured a horde streaming north to take away their jobs.

When you sit back and consider it, you can see that the people drawn to the GOP would have been northerners of just two kinds. The first would have been the rich. Bankers and merchants had nothing to fear from freeing the slaves. They knew they would retain their privileged position in any event. They were at liberty, so to speak, to act upon their indignation. The second would have been rural folk, the eighty percent or more of the northern population that lived on farms and in small towns. They were self-sufficient. They had no more fear of freeing the slaves than did the bankers and merchants. And it was just these two groups, the rich and the rural, that did indeed rally to the Republican Party.

Now, here is the odd part. The same two groups of northerners that provided much of the support for the Republican Party, the rich and the rural, also provided much of the support for the party that preceded the GOP, the Whig Party, and for the party that preceded the Whig Party, the Federalist Party. Yet when you compare their stands, you'll see that the Federalists, the Whigs, and the Republicans had virtually nothing in common.

The Federalists stood for a strong central government. Their party became defunct after the War of 1812. Then in the early 1830s the Whig Party emerged. Never managing to put together a coherent agenda of their own, the Whigs seldom stood for much of anything except animosity toward Andrew Jackson and the Democrats. The Whigs remained the second major party, in opposition to the Democrats (the descendants of Thomas Jefferson's Democratic-Republicans) for just over two decades. Then with the passage of the Kansas-Nebraska Act, the anti-slavery Whigs of the North, who dominated the party, found it impossible to cooperate with the pro-slavery Whigs of the South. The Whig Party collapsed. The GOP emerged, standing for abolition.

Three different parties: Federalists, Whigs, Republicans. Three different stands: in favor of a strong central government, against Andrew Jackson, in favor of abolition. Yet support from the same two groups of northerners sustained all three parties alike.

Both Versions One and Two inform the GOP to this day, as I've said. Version One, the version in which the Republican Party arose as a spontaneous moral protest, gives Republicans a certain pride. Once you recognize that the GOP was right on slavery, the greatest issue the nation ever faced, you can almost understand how Republicans manage to hold their heads high, even during a debacle such as the presidential campaign of Bob Dole.

Version Two establishes the existence of the Republican

tribe. Before it was the Republican tribe, of course, it was the Whig tribe, and before it was the Whig tribe, it was the Federalist tribe. Yet the tribe itself dates from the earliest years of the republic. Although the tribe has spread out, migrating from its original base in the North to other regions of the country, it exists to this day. Most Republicans are born into it—indeed, I learned, most Republicans are Republicans *because* they're born into it. This was not an idea that sat easily with me.

ME? A TRIBESMAN?

Journal entry:

In the library this afternoon, I came across the following passage. It's by the political scientist Judson L. James, writing in a book entitled American Party Politics.

> *Development of a partisan affiliation occurs early in the individual's socialization into political life. Except for the vaguest orientation toward government and governmental authority, and particularly the president, partisan identification is the earliest political attitude developed. . . .*
>
> *A person usually begins to regard himself as a Democrat or Republican before reaching voting age. . . . A party is evaluated well before one has any considerable amount of interest in or knowledge about politics. The "good guys" and the "bad guys" are largely defined by early associations: only later does one acquire a rationale for this choice.*

I found the passage infuriating.

"What are you so upset about?" David Brady asked. David's eyes are intensely blue. He fixed then on me.

"Tribal politics are the way America works," he continued. "I mean, look at you and me. I was born in an Irish neighborhood. My father worked in a factory. Everybody we knew sent their kids to parochial school, went to mass on Sunday, and had a picture of the pope in their kitchen. Membership in the Democratic Party might as well have been one more sacrament of the church.

"You? You grew up in a suburban town in upstate New York. I'm guessing here, but I'd bet all the fathers in your neighborhood had white-collar jobs, that everybody was of between one half and one hundred percent English extraction, and that on Sunday most of the families went to Presbyterian, Congregationalist, Methodist, or Episcopal churches. Am I right?"

I felt suddenly uncomfortable.

"That's more or less what the neighborhood was like," I admitted. "But that's not why we were Republicans."

David's eyes shone with amusement. "Don't tell me. Everybody in your neighborhood just happened to come to the same position on the issues."

"Something like that," I replied.

David laughed.

"Look, everybody in the neighborhood had a decent education," I said. "They thought things through. They were Republicans by choice."

David laughed again. "Let me ask you a question," he said. "What's your earliest memory of being a Republican?"

I thought about it for a moment. As soon as the memory came to me, I knew it would play into David's hands. But he was eyeing me. I had no choice. At the entrance of the Clayton Avenue Elementary School, I told him, rose a staircase divided by a brass handrail running down the middle. After their school buses dropped them off each morning in the autumn of 1964, the children who supported Johnson for president would go up one side of the staircase, the children who supported Goldwater up the other. I trudged up the Goldwater side. I have no idea how, but by the time I was in second grade I knew I was a Republican.

David roared with laughter. He slapped his knee. "I love it," he said. "A Republican by choice at the age of seven."

Why had I never before recognized the tribal character of the GOP? Thinking about it after my conversation with David Brady, I decided part of the reason involved the peculiarities of my own background. During my six years as a White House speechwriter, I had spent six or seven days a week researching issues and honing arguments. It had become firmly fixed in my mind that politics consisted of just that, issues and arguments. Republicans, I assumed, had given politics a great deal of thought. They had considered the issues. They had weighed the arguments. Then they had concluded that the GOP represented their own beliefs. In making this assumption I exhibited what the French call a *déformation professionnelle*. I had spent so much time writing speeches that I almost believed people were Republicans because Ronald Reagan and I had personally persuaded them.

The other part of the reason, I decided, was one of my many besetting sins, overweening pride. Me? A tribesman? Naturally I resisted the idea. It was so unflattering. Democrats as tribesmen? Now that was a notion I had no trouble with at all. I'm embarrassed to lay them out for you here, but I discovered I was carrying some ugly, half-formed thoughts in the back of my mind. Irish Catholics like David Brady, I believed, were one kind of people, while WASPs like me were another. The Irish—and for that matter, the Italians, the Slavs, and other immigrants—came to this country late. Ward bosses in city neighborhoods signed them up as Democrats by giving them turkeys for Christmas. They raised their children as Democrats because they didn't know any better. But us WASPs? We'd been in this country since the beginning. At home here, we were able to consider the issues carefully. We became Republicans because that's what thinking people do.

I was wrong. I grant it. I may not have liked the idea, but I was born a Republican just as surely as David Brady was born a Democrat.

Journal entry:

When I grew up, Vestal, New York, was a town of twenty thousand, overwhelmingly white, mostly Protestant. It was a good place, I see in retrospect, to raise children. The patterns of life were simple: The fathers worked while the mothers stayed home, and when one mother in the neighborhood had to go out to do the grocery shopping she could ask another to keep an eye on her kids. Everybody had a roomy house with a big yard. In the summer children would play tag, running up and down the front yards, while in the winter they would sled, packing snow and ice together to make a course through the backyards. Vestal was so middle-American that everybody actually thought our high school alma mater ("Along the rippling

Susquehanna/The shadow of our high school falls") con-
tained some pretty good poetry.

A couple of days ago I was trying to tell David Brady
that my hometown was a paragon of rationality, the habi-
tation of citizens who considered their politics with great
deliberation, supporting the Republican Party as a con-
scious act. Now I see that Vestal stood in direct line of de-
scent from the small towns throughout the North that
supported first the Federalists, then the Whigs, then the
Republicans. My hometown, a tribal encampment.

GO AHEAD, LOVE YOUR TRIBE

Yet even after I got used to the idea that I myself was born
into a tribe, the tribal nature of our political parties still troubled me. Americans were supposed to cast their ballots as
the result of a deliberative process, listening to opposing
points of view, then choosing the candidate that best represented their own conclusions. I may have overdone the importance of issues and arguments when I was in the White
House, but surely they had their place. Now I saw that most
Americans instead derived their predispositions to vote one
way or the other, Republican or Democratic, from their family background, their ethnicity, their religion—factors that
have nothing to do with a deliberative process.

"You're a political scientist," I said to Seymour Martin
Lipset over lunch. "Doesn't that pose a problem for political theory?"

Marty Lipset, who divides his time between George
Mason University and Stanford, is the author of *Political*

Man, first published in 1959 and still one of the basic texts of American political science. A big man with dark hair and dark eyes who loves to talk about political theory, Marty swatted a beefy hand through the air to wave my objection aside. "Sure it poses a problem," Marty replied. "If you buy the idea that every American is supposed to follow debates on television and clip newspaper articles on the candidates as if they were all members of the League of Women Voters. Thank God it *doesn't* work that way."

The political parties, Marty argued, provide the American system with stability and continuity. To do so, each of the parties must be able to rely upon large numbers of loyalists, supporters who will remain faithful to their party even when the party proves unpopular in the country at large.

"Look what happened when the Republicans got crushed by Franklin Roosevelt," Marty said. In 1932, the Republican Herbert Hoover lost the presidential election to the Democrat Franklin Roosevelt in a landslide. Four years later, in 1936, the Republican Alf Landon lost to Roosevelt in an even bigger landslide. "Tribal loyalties were the only reason the Republican Party managed to hang on at all," Marty said. The wealthy, managerial class and the small-town and rural populations of the Midwest and North continued to vote Republican, giving the GOP a base from which to rebuild.

"Now imagine it hadn't happened that way," Marty continued. "Imagine that even the bankers and farmers forgot about their loyalties to the GOP and just asked themselves who seemed like the more attractive candidate, Hoover or Roosevelt in 1932 or Landon or Roosevelt in 1936." The Republican defeats would have been even worse. The GOP would have suffered such massive defections that it would have effectively ceased to exist.

"After that, the Democrats would have faced nothing more than token opposition from a lot of scattered little groups," Marty said. There would have been no continuing debate over the New Deal, no organized and sustained critique of Franklin Roosevelt's foreign policy. It would not have been long before the Democrats, enjoying absolute power, would have demonstrated the truth of Lord Acton's famous dictum, becoming corrupted absolutely. To name just one abuse, Franklin Roosevelt would have been able to get away with his notorious 1937 scheme to pack the Supreme Court. The system of checks and balances the founders devised would have been substantially overturned.

It occurred to me that Marty was overstating his case. That was fine by me. He was making an interesting point. But Marty must have detected some skepticism on my face. "Look," he said, waving his hand again, "I hope you don't think this hypothetical. It isn't. All you have to do is look at Russia."

Russia—lawless, corrupt, bankrupt, violent, and without any foreseeable prospect of climbing out of the mess that it's in. Marty argued that a big part of the trouble is that Russia lacks a two-party system. "The only stable party is the Communist Party, which gets about a quarter to a third of the vote. The other parties are ad-hoc groupings based on personalities." There are Putin people. There are Primakov people. But there are no large, enduring political entities that can grapple with issues independently of this or that strong-man. In the parliamentary election of 1999, two of the parties were formed only weeks before the elections took place. "Those two parties came up from zero," Marty said. "Any time you've got parties popping up like that you've got a very unstable and dangerous situation." We keep hearing about how the Russians need a stable currency and more secure property rights. Those wouldn't be a bad idea, Marty admitted. "But you know what the Russians could really use? A couple of functioning political parties."

Political parties keep the American system stable—and tribal loyalties keep the parties stable. Seeking, so to speak, a second opinion, I presented Marty Lipset's argument to David Brady. David subscribed to it himself. "As far as I'm concerned," David said, "every American should get down on his knees every night and thank God that people like the Irish are loyal to the Democratic Party while people like you WASPs can't stop being Republican even if you try."

In turning to the Republican past, I had of course expected to learn something about GOP history. What I hadn't counted on was quite so many lessons in humility.

First I discovered that I was ignorant. I had supposed the GOP was formed in opposition to slavery. Strictly speaking, I was correct. But I knew nothing of the continuity among the Republican, Whig, and Federalist parties. What would come to be known as the Republican Party formed not in the middle of the nineteenth century but in the earliest days of the nation's existence. Membership has been handed down as it is handed down in all tribes—unconsciously. I cannot recall how I became a Republican. When I checked with him, neither could my older brother, Don. "I had blue eyes and brown hair and I was a Republican," my brother said. "It was always just part of my identity."

Then I discovered that although I had always looked down on people who don't take their politics seriously, the GOP relies on them. When you think about it, who *could* live up to the standards the founders implied in the Constitution? The document is so rational, deliberate, and prudent. George Washington may have embodied all those qualities. Few others have even come close. Yet the very institutions the founders failed to take into account, our political parties, manage to mediate between Americans as they actually are—impatient, busy, never more than half interested in politics—and the alabaster coolness of the document by which the founders expected us to live. The preppie on the golf course who can't name his congressman and the jock who would rather watch a football game than a presidential debate are just as useful to the Republican Party as I am—maybe more so. The GOP can always count on them. I take politics so seriously that if somebody founded a crackpot Reagan Party, I'd actually be tempted to break with the GOP to join it.

I even got a lesson in humility toward Democrats.

A couple of comments he had dropped over the years had led me to suspect that my cousin Dave was himself a Democrat. When I called him, he confirmed it. "I've been a Democrat all my life," he said. I asked Dave for his earliest political memory.

"The year was 1964," Dave replied after thinking for a moment. "Robert Kennedy was running for the Senate in New York State. There was a reception for Kennedy in Rochester, and my mom went. She heard him speak. Afterward she got the chance to shake his hand. I can remember her coming home and telling us how impressed she was." The very year that I was trudging up the Goldwater side of my elementary school staircase, my cousin was listening to his mother extol the virtues of a Kennedy.

"Dave, do you think of yourself as English or Irish?" Although Dave's father, my own father's brother, Uncle Ken, is of entirely English descent, Dave's mother, Aunt Rita, born Rita Kelly, is of entirely Irish descent.

"Irish," Dave replied. "There's no question about it. Mom was a big one for Irishness. I can remember St. Patrick's Day in parochial school. Every year Mom sent my brother and me to school in little green bow ties."

My cousin Dave, Irish Catholic—and a Democrat. I had always thought Democrats were either willfully ignorant or perverse. What other explanation could there be? Now I knew. Like Dave, people could be Democrats to honor the ways of their own tribe.

Chapter Three

To Live and Die in Dixie

Journal entry:

The South may be the new Republican heartland, but it still feels foreign to me. Taking off from Atlanta not long ago, I noticed that the city's skyline contains as much glimmering glass and steel as that of Boston. Then I made the mistake of continuing to gaze out the window as the plane gained altitude. Outside Atlanta and its immediate suburbs, as far as I could tell, lies nothing but acre upon acre of scrub trees and red dirt. When I tried to imagine what life must be like down there, I found myself humming "Dueling Banjos" from the movie Deliverance.

QUESTION: What do you call the hillbillies who appeared in *Deliverance*?

ANSWER: Fellow Republicans.

All right. I'm being unfair. But the reader may as well know that in looking at the South, I'll be starting out as a skeptic.

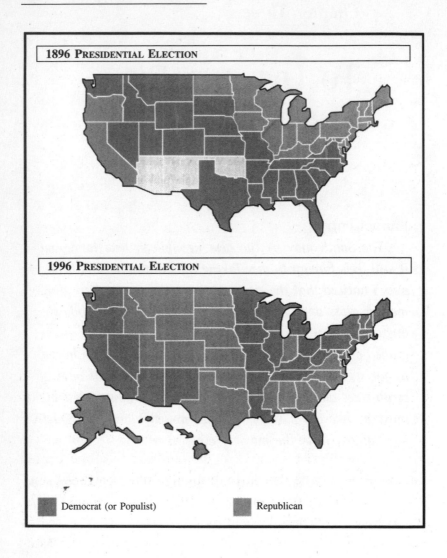

1896 PRESIDENTIAL ELECTION

1996 PRESIDENTIAL ELECTION

Democrat (or Populist)   Republican

In the last several decades a curious event took place in American politics. It might be termed the Big Switch. The Republican Party, which used to be based in the North, has swapped bases with the Democratic Party, which used to be based in the South and the Rocky Mountains. The Big Switch was so pronounced that, as the map indicates, voting patterns in the presidential elections of 1896, before the Switch began, and of 1996, after the Switch was complete, amount to mirror images of each other. The change in the South has been especially dramatic: Dixie, which used to be the most reliably Democratic region in the nation, has become rock-solid for the GOP.

After learning that the region in which I grew up, the North, used to be the stronghold of the GOP, it made sense to look next at the region that is the stronghold of the GOP today. You might think that Republicans would be delighted to have conquered the Old Confederacy. Yet it turns out that there are some very shrewd Republicans who almost wish the Democrats had kept the South to themselves.

THE BIG SWITCH

The transformation of the South into Republican territory is actually the last part of the Big Switch. The North went Democratic first. The trend in the North began more than a century ago, during the great wave of immigration to the United States from Europe that lasted roughly from the 1880s until the enactment of strict quotas in 1924. Irish, Italians, Jews, Poles, Slavs, Scandinavians, and other immigrants settled in the cities of the Northeast and, to a lesser extent, the Midwest. By 1910, three-quarters of the inhabitants of New York, Chicago, Cleveland, Detroit, and Boston were first- or second-generation immigrants. As far back as the eighteenth century the Democratic Party had attracted the support of workers in northern cities. Now the numbers of workers in northern cities expanded dramatically. It often took one or two generations for the new immigrants to become regular voters. But when they did vote, they voted Democratic. The North went Democratic simply because so many Democrats moved in.

The Rocky Mountain states participated in the Big Switch by going Republican during the last several decades, at roughly the same time as the South. The region's original inhabitants were of two kinds. The first was farmers and ranchers. The second was silver miners. Both voted Democratic because the Democrats—notably under the three-time Democratic presidential candidate, William Jennings Bryan—sought a currency based on silver rather than gold. A silver regime would have required the federal government to make massive new purchases of silver, thereby profiting the miners, while in effect inflating the currency, thereby profiting debtors, such as the farmers and ranchers, who borrowed heavily to bring livestock and equipment into the region. When the Rockies were developed after the Second World War, the population of the region expanded. Quickly outnumbering the thin Democratic population, the new arrivals tended to come more often from the Midwest and South, the first of which was already Republican, the second of which would soon be Republican, than from the urban Democratic strongholds of the Great Lakes and the Northeast. When they reached the Rockies, they found a constellation of special circumstances that nurtured Republican loyalties. Much of the land in the Rockies, for example, was, as it still is, owned by the federal government—in Idaho and Utah the proportion of land owned by the federal government is well over half. This prompts resentment of the federal government and a correspondingly favorable outlook on the anti–big government GOP. Hunting, to name a second example, is popular throughout the Rockies. This leads to high rates of gun ownership and, once again, a favorable outlook on the GOP, which through the years has devoted a great deal of energy to beating back Democratic gun control proposals. Add a growing Mormon population—Mormons, whose beliefs stress traditional morality, represent the most Republican religious denomination in the country—and you end up with a Republican stripe running from Idaho to Arizona.

This brings us to the South.

EATING PEAS

To understand why the South became Republican, you need to understand why it was Democratic in the first place. The answer, of course, is the Civil War.

At an event not long ago I found myself seated next to Marianne Gingrich, the second wife of former Speaker of the House Newt Gingrich. (She is now the former wife of the former Speaker, but when this took place Newt Gingrich had not yet divorced Marianne.) A striking, dark-haired woman, Marianne mentioned that she had grown up in Ohio. I asked what it had been like to move to the South in the early 1980s when she married Gingrich, who at the time represented a suburb of Atlanta. She replied that it had proven a shock.

"In Ohio," Marianne said, "you had the big cities—Cleveland, Dayton, Columbus—where people voted Democratic. But then you had other cities that were mixed—Cincinnati was more Republican, and Canton wasn't too Democratic. And then you had the countryside, where the farmers lived, and that was very Republican. When I moved to Georgia I found out that where you lived didn't matter. It just didn't matter. You could live in a city or you could live on a farm, and you were a Democrat either way.

"I know people who still can't pick up a Republican registration form," Marianne said. "I mean, the physical act is beyond them. It would be a betrayal of their parents and grandparents. The Civil War was alive and well when I moved to Georgia, I can tell you that."

The Civil War, alive and well in Georgia as recently as the early 1980s? When I grew up in upstate New York twenty years earlier, the Civil War was just one more topic in history class. What accounted for the difference? To the extent that I had thought about it, I realized, I had always assumed the Civil War lingered in southern memory simply because the South had lost. Losers are always engaging in wistful examinations of the ways things might have turned out differently. Then I spent some time back in the library. "Wistful," I learned, was the wrong word for the way that southerners felt about the Civil War. Right up until the most recent one or two generations of southerners, better words would have been "embittered" and "irate."

It is a truism that the Civil War was harder on the South than on the North. But as truisms go, this one is especially true. Whereas most of the states in the North never caught so much as a glimpse of a confederate army—minor raids aside, no confederate action ever penetrated any farther north than Gettysburg, Pennsylvania—all eleven states in the South saw Union invasions. The destruction in the South was staggering. Miles of railway line were ripped up. Swaths of countryside were denuded. Virtually every major southern city came under attack. Charleston was bombarded. Vicksburg was starved into submission. Richmond was besieged, then ransacked. Atlanta was burned to the ground. As a proportion of its white population, the South suffered more than two-and-a-half times as many men killed and wounded as did the

North. For decades afterward the southern countryside was littered with ghostly plantation houses and hamlets to which men had never come home. The Civil War inflicted on the South a catastrophe of the proportions of an Old Testament plague or a medieval epidemic.

Then came Reconstruction.

The South was divided into military districts and occupied by federal troops. The troops stayed for more than a decade. Overriding the wishes of President Andrew Johnson, who, himself a southerner, was disposed to treat the South leniently, Congress imposed new constitutions on the southern states, then passed one law after another intended to eradicate all that remained of the old South while creating a new South intended to look just like the North. Officeholders in the new state governments were almost entirely of just three kinds: freed slaves, carpetbaggers (northerners who had moved South to exploit southerners), and scalawags (southern collaborators).

Invaded and devastated during the Civil War. Occupied and humiliated during Reconstruction. Whom was the South to blame? That was an easy one. The Republican Party. The Republican Party had made Lincoln president and done his bidding in pursuing the Civil War. (For a time during the Civil War itself, the Republican Party renamed itself the Union Party. A bid for the support of pro-Union Democrats, the ploy fooled no one and was soon dropped.) Then, acting through its majority in Congress, the Republican Party had imposed a vengeful, draconian Reconstruction. If you were a white southerner in the last couple of decades of the nineteenth century, calling yourself a Republican would have been like spitting on the grave of every southern boy who had fallen to a Yankee bullet and every southern woman who had starved to death after the Yankees freed her slaves. You had no choice. You called yourself a Democrat.

Only two groups insisted on calling themselves Republicans instead. One was made up of whites in the Appalachian back country. They worked small farms on marginal land. Seldom slave owners, they had little in common with the planters of the coastal South and had opposed secession—indeed, opposition to secession had proven so fierce in the back country of Virginia that Lincoln had been able to split dozens of counties from the state, recognizing them in 1863 as the new state of West Virginia. The other group was of course made up of freed slaves. Looking on the Republican Party with understandable gratitude, black people became Republican en masse. Since restrictions imposed by the Republican Congress denied the vote to tens of thousands of whites—in some locations, half of white voters found themselves disenfranchised—the black vote enabled Republicans to dominate state governments throughout the South.

How did the Democratic white majority deal with these two groups of dissidents? During Reconstruction, it took the law into its own hands. Since it saw its own state governments as mere puppets for the Republicans in Congress, it considered itself justified in doing so. White southerners formed organizations such as the Ku Klux Klan and the Knights of the White Camelia, intimidating black people and pressuring back-country whites to conform with the white majority.

When, with the withdrawal of the last federal troops in 1877, Reconstruction at last ended, the white establishment reasserted itself, swiftly reclaiming political power. While in 1872 nine of the eleven states of the Old Confederacy had Republican governors, by 1880 eleven of eleven had Democratic governors. To the crude informal means of controlling their political opponents that the Klan and the Knights represented, the white establishment now added crude formal means, enacting poll taxes and literacy requirements that effectively removed the vote from black people and poor whites alike.

Throughout the Old Confederacy, the Democratic Party thus became a monolith, the sole acceptable outlet for political life. In the words of the historian W. J. Cash, the Democratic Party

> ceased to be a party *in* the South and became the party *of* the South, a kind of confraternity having in its keeping the whole corpus of Southern loyalties, and so irresistibly commanding the allegiance of faithful whites that to doubt it, to question it in any detail, was *ipso facto* to stand branded as a renegade to race, to country, to God, and to Southern Womanhood.

The Solid South. Loyalty to the Democratic Party was handed down from parent to child along with the family photograph albums and the Civil War mementos.

A friend of mine, Barry Germany, has lived nearly all his life in Meridian, Mississippi. When I telephoned to ask him about the Civil War and Reconstruction, Barry immediately replied with some family history. (I have some family history involving the Civil War, too—a great-great-uncle of mine fought for the North—but I never even knew it until I started asking my mother questions for this book. Yankees that we were, we never paid much attention to the Civil War.) "My mother's great-grandmother was born in 1845," Barry told me. "After Sherman destroyed Meridian in 1863, her children had nothing to eat. Some slaves found peas in a field. The children were given the immature peas to eat. The grown-ups boiled and ate the pods. Those were very hard days. Down here, there's not a family that doesn't remember them."

That story—and the resentment toward Republicans that goes with it—has been passed down in Barry's family for five generations. The first three generations were Democrats.

The last two, Barry's parents and Barry himself, are Republicans.

GEOR-UDGE, I KNEW YOUR DADDY

To my mind, the person who best represents the new, Republican Dixie is a friend of mine named Haley Barbour. Haley, fifty-one, a stocky, round-faced man with a big grin, grew up in Yazoo City, Mississippi. (If an invading force of Martians ever wanted a reliable way to tell northerners and southerners apart, all they'd have to do is mention Yazoo City. When they hear the name, northerners like me can't help smirking. Southerners like Haley don't see anything funny about it at all.) When he was a very young man Haley defected from the Democratic Party in which he had been raised to become active in the Mississippi Republican Party, and by the time he was in his twenties he had been elected chairman of the Mississippi GOP. At the same time, the early 1970s, climbing to the top of the Mississippi GOP seemed an improbable way to launch a career in politics. Democrats so dominated Mississippi that as far as I can discover there were only four lonely Republican officeholders in the entire state: two members out of 122 in the state assembly, and two members out of 52 in the state senate. Yet just over two decades later, Mississippi had a congressional delegation in which Republicans outnumbered Democrats, a Republican governor for the first time since Reconstruction, and a reputation for voting solidly Republican in presidential elections. Haley had a lot to do with the transformation—even after stepping down as chairman he remained one of the leaders of the Mississippi GOP. In Republican circles Haley became so famous that in 1992 President George Bush named him the chairman of the Republican National Committee, making Haley the highest-ranking Republican in the country after the president himself. Haley played a central role in the election of 1994, in which the GOP won back the House of Representatives for the first time in four decades, a feat the party accomplished in large part by picking up nineteen new seats in the South. After stepping down as party chairman, Haley opened a law firm in Washington. But he remains so devoted to the South that he commutes back to Yazoo City (that name again) every weekend. When I wanted to ask an expert how the old, Democratic South became the new, Republican South, I called Haley.

Haley and I began our conversation the way we begin every conversation, with a few jokes about the event at which we first met. "That was one *hail* of a speech you wrote," Haley said, chuckling. "Damn near got me elected."

The story is worth telling. It amounts, so to speak, to a snapshot of the South partway through its transformation.

The year was 1982. Haley, then just 34, was running for the United States Senate against the Democratic incumbent, John Stennis. On the staff of then Vice President George Bush, I was with the vice president when he flew to Jackson, Mississippi, to appear at an enormous rally on Haley's behalf. Soon after I reached my room in the hotel in which the vice president and his party were staying, my telephone rang. It was the vice president's press secretary, Pete Teeley. He was with the vice president. "Get down here right away," Pete said. When I reached the vice president's suite, Pete let me in. George Bush was seated with his feet propped on a coffee table. He looked grumpy. "The vice president would like to know why we're in Jackson," Pete said.

This seemed an odd question. I was just twenty-six, the most junior member of the staff. My job was to take the speech assignments as they were given to me and do the best with each one that I could. I had nothing to do with putting events on the vice president's schedule.

"The vice president is here to give a speech for someone called Haley Barbour," I said. "Barbour is running for the Senate."

Pete looked disgusted. "We know *that* much," he replied. "But *why*?"

I ransacked my memory. Had anyone back in Washington told me anything special about the stop in Jackson? All I could come up with was a conversation I'd had with John Morgan, who worked across the hall from me in the Old Executive Office Building. John was on the president's staff, not the vice president's, so strictly speaking there was never any reason for us to talk. But since our offices were so close we had become friends. John's job was to provide the president's staff with political advice. On the walls of his office hung a set of enormous maps of the United States. John had colored the maps by hand to show the county-by-county results of each presidential race going back more than a century. When I had stopped by John's office to shoot the breeze not long before, I had happened to mention that the vice president would be flying to Mississippi to give a speech for the Republican Senate candidate. "Nobody can beat Senator Stennis," John had replied. A member of the Senate since 1947, John explained, Stennis was a southern institution. "The only reason to go down to Mississippi is because Senator Stennis is old now. Bush will just be showing the flag for the local GOP, giving them a little moral support to tide them over until the day when Senator Stennis finally steps down."

John Morgan had just been engaging in casual banter, whereas I was being asked to brief the vice president of the United States. But the conversation I had had with John was all that I could come up with.

"The vice president is just here to show the flag," I said. Then I repeated the rest of what John had told me.

George Bush and Pete Teeley exchanged looks of relief. Then the vice president told me what was going on.

"I just got a call from Senator Stennis," Bush said. He lapsed into a pretty good imitation of a Mississippi drawl. " 'Now Geor-udge,' " Bush said, quoting Stennis, " 'I used to know your daddy. He and I were good friends right heah in the Senate. [George Bush's father, Prescott Bush, represented Connecticut in the Senate from 1952 to 1963.] Why, ah re-membuh your daddy fondly. And it huhts me to think that his son would go into my home state to campaign against me. Ah'm with y'all, Geor-udge. Ah'm with you an' prez-dent Reagan. There's no need for y'all to be sayin' things against me. Not me who knew your daddy and has voted with you and prez-dent Reagan right along.'

"So," the vice president said, dropping the southern accent, "if I'm just here to show the flag, that's all I intend to do."

Two hours later, in front of a crowd of several thousand cheering Mississippians, Haley Barbour introduced the vice president. George Bush strode to the lectern, relaxed and smil-ing. For the next twenty minutes he delivered the speech just as I had written it—with one difference. Since the vice president was there to speak on behalf of Haley Barbour, I had of course composed several paragraphs in praise of Haley, talking about Haley's modest upbringing in Yazoo City, his rise to the chairmanship of the Mississippi GOP, his patriotism, his vision, his so on and so forth. The vice president dropped them. He never even mentioned Haley's name. He went directly from the grand traditions of the South to the greatness of Ronald Reagan with no Haley Barbour in between. Haley stood next to the vice president throughout the speech. As he kept waiting to hear himself mentioned, his smile grew strained. When he heard the vice president close, saying, "Thank you, God bless you, and God bless the great state of Mississippi," it was all Haley could do to keep even a strained smile on his face. The vice president waved to the crowd, then left the stage before anyone could ask him to pose with Haley for photographs. Mississippi had given the 1980 Republican presidential and vice presidential candidates, Ronald Reagan and George Bush, the biggest plurality they received in any state. But in the person of Senator Stennis the old, Democratic South lived on, and not even the vice president of the United States cared to mess with it. On election day, Haley Barbour lost to John Stennis in a landslide.

HOW THE SOUTH CHANGED

"You want to know how the South turned Republican?" Haley asked. "Then go get a copy of the book by the Black brothers." Earl and Merle Black are the authors of *Politics and Society in the South*. (Distinguished political scientists, the brothers are twins who grew up in the South. Their first names amount to another one of those tests that Martians could use to tell northerners and southerners apart. To my Yankee ears, twins named Earl and Merle sound hopelessly hick. But when I tried to explain this to my southern friend Haley, he couldn't understand what I meant.) I got a copy of the Black brothers' book and worked my way through it. According to Earl and Merle Black and my friend Haley Barbour, the South went Republican because Yankees moved in, the economy of the South finally began to expand, and a new generation of southerners got sick of having Democrats run everything.

Why did Yankees move in? To escape the snowy winters and high cost of living of the North, to serve in the armed forces at one of the dozens of military bases located in the South, and to manage the new factories that were turning the land of cotton into the land of manufactured goods. They arrived in such large numbers that while in 1920 the proportion of white southerners born outside the South—in a word, Yankees—was under one in ten, by 1980 the proportion had risen to one in five. Now, it happens that the three kinds of Yankees who moved South—retirees, members of the military, and managers—are as Republican as any three demographic groups you could name. The Old Confederacy might as well have established a border patrol, permitting only Republicans to enter. Of the three groups, the managers are Haley's favorites. They get involved in party activities. They give money to GOP candidates. They're not just Republicans, they're useful Republicans.

"We had a whole *lot* of managers and executives move down South," Haley told me. "Look at the suburbs of Atlanta. You show me a neighborhood so new that the grass hadn't come up yet in the yard and I'll bet you those people are going to be Republican. That's the way it is all *over* the

South. You'll find the best and most useful Republicans where there's the newest grass."

While the Yankees were moving in, the southern economy was expanding. The expansion took the form of almost entirely industrial growth. While in 1920 agriculture accounted for half of jobs in the South but only a fifth of jobs outside the South, by 1970 the South had roughly the same rate of agricultural employment as the rest of the country. Industry had moved in. As the South became industrial, the old, landed white families that had formed the core of the Democratic establishment grew unimportant. A new middle class arose. In the North, many of these new middle-class workers would have joined unions, which are overwhelmingly Democratic. In the South, there were scarcely any unions to be found. An outgrowth of industrial development, which the region had never before experienced, unions had failed to become established in the South. Now that industrial development was at last taking place, southern workers, who knew why they were being given a chance at industrial jobs—"Hell," Haley explained, "getting away from unions is why industry went down there"—were content to remain unorganized. Without unions to tie the southern middle class to the Democratic Party, the southern middle class votes Republican.

This brings us to the third trend. While Yankees were moving in and a new, industrial economy was springing up, young southerners were getting sick of the old Democratic system. A generation of hotheads arose, just as intent on causing trouble as their great-grandfathers had been when they went raiding with Jeb Stuart. Haley found himself at the center of this trend, no doubt because he did so much to foment it. "Folks my age joined the Republican Party because it was the reform party, the party of change, the party of kickin' out the folks who'd been runnin' things down at the courthouse for generations." In Mississippi this group included not only Haley himself but Trent Lott, who was elected to the Senate in 1988 when John Stennis at last retired and has served the last four years as Senate majority leader. Haley quoted his old friend Trent. "Trent used to say—now, this was twenty years ago, and you'd never catch him saying it today—Trent used to say, 'Hell, if the Republicans had been in office down here for a hundred years, I might've become a Democrat just to run *them* off.' "

One question had to be asked. When the South went Republican, what role had race played?

"Just about none," Haley replied.

The GOP has scrupulously avoided any taint of racism. "No Republican candidate could get elected in the South if he was perceived as a racist," Haley said. "No way. Not a chance. There is just a huge part of the GOP that runs away from a candidate if there are *any* charges that he's a racist." When the racist David Duke announced that he intended to run for governor of Louisiana as a Republican, for instance, prominent Republicans across the South denounced him. "Our party," Haley continued, "is real middle class." The GOP does not belong to rednecks and bigots, in other words, but to young managers like those you see trying to get their grass to grow outside Atlanta.

If Haley and the Black brothers had a theme, it was change. The New South was just that, new. The South had become Republican because it had become more industrial, more middle class, more Yankee-fied. Yet I thought I saw a second reason. The South had become Republican because it hadn't changed.

HOW THE SOUTH REMAINED THE SAME

Yankee-fication? Millions of Yankees have indeed moved south. But they have tended to cluster together. In northern Virginia, there are so many Yankees among the government workers who commute across the Potomac each morning to Washington, D.C., that if you picked the region up and put it down someplace else, most of the residents would feel more at home in New Jersey or Connecticut than elsewhere in Virginia. In South Florida, Yankees outnumber the natives, and in the long coastal crescent from Key West to Miami to West Palm Beach you're more likely to hear the accents of the Midwest or New York than of Dixie. But outside these Yankee clusters genuine southerners still predominate. As recently as 1981, Yankees made up less than a tenth of the population in 750 of the Old Confederacy's 1,145 counties.

Industrialization? True, the South is a great deal more industrial today than it was as little as one or two decades ago. Yet even now much of Dixie remains heavily agricultural. Put yourself in the middle of the most industrialized, Yankee neighborhood in the South that you can find. You still won't have to drive more than an hour to find a place where farming continues to be the main source of income and Yankees remain rare. (Even in Yankee clusters, it's a good question whether the northerners have more influence on the southerners who surround them or the other way around. My cousin, Tom, and his wife, Marsha, moved from New York to a suburb of Memphis when their children were little. Now adults, all three children speak with a Tennessee accent and root for Ole Miss.)

In spite of all the changes it has undergone, the South remains a place set apart, possessed of its own culture, different from every part of the country. I suspect that two distinctively southern traits in particular had a lot to do with the region's entry into the Republican fold. I learned about the traits from books, not firsthand experience. But they fit with everything I know about the South. Both traits go back—far back. According to David Hackett Fischer, the author of *Albion's Seed,* a study of colonial America, they date from at least the seventeenth century. The first is a love of the military.

As Fischer explains, the first settlers in the South were comprised of two groups. One was aristocrats, displaced after the Puritans defeated Charles I. The other was border-country people, inhabitants of the fierce, lawless regions between England and Scotland. Each brought with it a military tradition. They bequeathed their love of the military to the entire region.

While at the outbreak of the Civil War the North possessed few military academies, the South was dotted with them (including the Virginia Military Institute, or VMI, which became famous a few years ago when a court ordered it to go co-ed and it at first resisted). And during the Civil War itself, as Fischer writes, "the south was superior to the north in the intensity of its warrior ethic." When a Yankee like me looks at Pickett's charge, the exposed Confederate advance across open fields at Gettysburg, he sees only slaughter. Plenty of southerners I know see gallantry.

Even today the southern military tradition remains powerful. The nation's armed forces draws a disproportionately large number of officers from the South, and at one point during the 1980s the South boasted an astonishing ninety-one military bases, more than any other region. When the Democratic Party adopted a dovish stance during the Vietnam War, southerners found the stance offensive—George McGovern, the Democratic presidential candidate in 1972, lost worse in the South than in any other region—while finding the Republican emphasis on national strength correspondingly attractive.

The second trait is regional pride.

Derived, like love of the military, from the first settlers in the South, this trait precipitated the Civil War. Even after he was elected president, after all, Lincoln promised to protect slavery where it already existed, merely preventing its expansion into new territory. If it had accepted these terms, the South could have preserved its way of life, conceivably for decades. Yet, as Fischer writes, "The Republican victory [of Lincoln] was seen . . . as an affront to southern honor."

A century later the affront to southern honor arose from forced integration, rising taxes, proliferating federal regulations—in a word, from the Democratic Party and its Great Society. (The Great Society may have been launched by a southerner, President Lyndon Johnson of Texas, but the principal support for the program came from up North.) The South disliked getting pushed around by northern liberals almost as much as it had disliked getting pushed around by northern abolitionists.

Steeped in military tradition and a sense of regional honor, the culture of the South is thus a conservative culture. Southerners still put their hands over their hearts when they sing the national anthem. For that matter they still know the words to the national anthem. They look up to veterans and down on federal bureaucrats. They've gotten used to hearing the rest of the country snicker at them, resigning themselves to it as the price they have to pay to preserve their ways. But let the rest of the country start ordering them around, in the person of a federal judge or an official of the Environmental Protection Agency, and southerners will bristle. Sooner or later people like that were bound to start voting Republican.

My friend Barry Germany summed it up. When I told him about all the changes in the South that Haley and the Black brothers cited, Barry replied, "That may all be true. But the reason the South went Republican seems simpler to me. The Democratic Party just got to be too liberal for folks down here."

Although at the state and local level, the South remains largely Democratic—the legislatures of nine of the eleven states of the Old Confederacy remain in the control of Democrats—in national politics, the South has been reliably Republican for nearly three decades. The Old Confederacy has supported the Republican presidential candidate in every election since 1968 except one, the election of 1976, when it voted for the southerner, Jimmy Carter, over the northerner, Gerald Ford, but even then by a modest margin. From 1980 onward, the South has given Republican presidential candidates larger margins than has any other region of the country, including the Rocky Mountains. Even in 1996, when the Republican presidential nominee was Bob Dole, the least compelling Republican candidate since Alf Landon, the South stuck with the GOP, permitting Dole to sweep the region, not that it did him much good. In Congress, too, the GOP reflects the disproportionate support it receives from its southern base. Although the South accounts for just 20 percent of the country's population, in 1998 it sent to Congress 39 percent of all House Republicans.

If when I was a boy the GOP's favorite anthem was "The

Battle Hymn of the Republic," today the GOP is whistling "Dixie."

Not everyone cares for the tune.

DIXIE CONTRA MUNDUM

Journal entry:

Today I played a word-association game with a friend who, because he has in-laws in the South, wishes to remain anonymous. I named regions of the country. He replied with the first few words or phrases that came to mind.

"New England," I said.

"Foliage in the fall," he replied. "Covered bridges. Maple syrup."

"The Midwest."

"Farmland," he replied. "Good-hearted, plain-spoken people."

"The West."

"Palm trees," he answered. "Beaches. High tech. Hollywood."

"The South."

"The South?" my friend said. "Oh, I see what you're getting at. Big fat motorcycle cops with mirrored sunglasses, waiting to pull guys over. Televangelists ripping off widows by getting them to send in their Social Security checks. Hillbillies so inbred they have six fingers on each hand. Girls with big hair, big boobs, and no brains. You want me to keep going?"

It amounted to a concise illustration of the problem.

There is a school of thought that the South is bad for the GOP. The South, this school holds, is too pro-gun and pro-military, produces abrasive leaders in Congress, such as Congressman Dick Armey and Tom DeLay of Texas and Senator Jesse Helms of North Carolina, and generally accents its politics the way it accents its speech—in a way that jars on everybody outside the South. Worst of all, the South is the home of the religious right.

The argument was best stated in an article that appeared not long ago in the *Atlantic Monthly*. The article disturbed me, partly because it was entitled "Why the GOP is Doomed," and partly because it was written by the journalist Christopher Caldwell, whom I know to be an astute political observer. "There is a big problem with having a southern, as opposed to a Midwestern or a California, base," Caldwell wrote.

> Southern interests diverge from those of the rest of the country, and the southern presence in the Republican Party has passed the "tipping point" and begun to alienate voters from other regions.

> The most profound clash between the South and everyone else, of course, is a cultural one. It arises from the southern tradition of putting values—particularly Christian ones—at the center of politics ... [Non-southerners] are put off to see that "traditional" values are now defined by the majority party as the values of ... denizens of two-year-old churches and three-year-old shopping malls.

Televangelist Jerry Falwell's Moral Majority may now be defunct—Falwell shut down the controversial organization in

1996—but the majority in the South still likes to think of it-self as moral. When that attitude gets mixed up with politics, the anti-southern school believes, it strikes everybody outside the South as sanctimonious.

I grant the observation—Republicans in the South do indeed place moral values smack in the middle of their politics. On the Web site of the Republican Party of Texas, for example, you'll find a page that contrasts the beliefs of Republicans with those of Democrats. "Republicans," the page asserts,

> believe the traditional family and the values it fosters are the foundation of American society and their preservation is essential to our Nation's continued success. Democrats believe American society must redefine its values and the role of the family to fit new lifestyle concepts, which have resulted from the 60s counter-culture movement.

If "good people" had been substituted for "Republicans," while "sinners," "reprobates," or "degenerates" had been substituted for "Democrats," that passage could have been preached from any one of a thousand pulpits across the South. As a mandate for policy, the passage is so vague that it can be read as calling for everything from revisions in the federal tax code (an end to the marriage penalty, perhaps, or an extension of the child care credit to mothers who remain at home) to new state laws regulating divorce (an attempt to strengthen the institution of marriage by repealing no-fault divorce statutes). Yet its moral stance is clear. The correct setting in which to raise children is that of a marriage between a man and a woman. Same-sex marriages, the adoption of children by homosexuals—these are to be opposed.

This stance does indeed make many outside the South—even many Republicans—queasy. In California as I write, signatures are being gathered to place the Protection of Marriage Initiative on the ballot. The initiative would define marriage as a strictly heterosexual union. Yet although the California Republican Party has endorsed the measure, leading members of the Party, including Congressman Tom Campbell, who is running for the Senate, have denounced it.

"Republicans," the Texas GOP asserts further down the Web site page, "believe human life is sacred and worthy of protection. Democrats believe there should be no restrictions on abortion."

This passage, too, leaves a great deal to conjecture. Does it represent a call to outlaw abortion outright? Or to make exceptions in cases of rape and incest? Yet the passage's pro-life tenor is of course unmistakable. It is also out of keeping with opinion—even Republican opinion—in much of the country outside the South. In the Northeast, Republican governors George Pataki of New York, Christine Todd Whitman of New Jersey, John Rowland of Connecticut, and Tom Ridge of Pennsylvania are all pro-choice, as is Pete Wilson, the former Republican governor of California, in the West.

I grant, as I've said, that Republicans in the South place moral values smack in the middle of their politics. Yet the more I think about it, the more I admire them for doing just that.

Journal entry:
A synopsis of the evening:
Edita [my wife] tried to get the three boys to bed on her own while I sat on the piano bench next to our eight-year-old daughter, listening to her practice the C-major scale,

her tiny fingers, their fingernails encrusted with dirt, work-ing their way up and down the keys. The boys refused to settle down. Edita asked me to put my head in their room. I found the two-and-a-half-year-old attempting to climb the bunk bed to disturb the six-year-old, pulled the two-and-a-half-year-old off the bunk bed to place him, wriggling, in his own bed, then noticed that the four-year-old, in the bot-tom bunk, was gesturing to me, bent to put my ear next to his lips, heard him ask for a glass of water, went to the kitchen, got the water, and returned to discover that the six-year-old had begun to sob, having just remembered that during his kindergarten nature walk this afternoon—that is, some six hours before—he had fallen and scraped his knee.

I went back to the kitchen, searched in a drawer for a Band-Aid, then returned to the boys' room to put the Band-Aid on the six-year-old's knee, only to have him inform me, snuffling back tears, that he needed two Band-Aids, not one. I went back to the kitchen yet again. As I riffled through the drawer, searching for a second Band-Aid, I could hear that instead of continuing to practice her C-major scale, as I had instructed, our daughter had skipped ahead to the right-hand part of "Camptown Races." Although she was hitting most of the right notes, I knew that she was mak-ing up her fingering as she went along, learning the piece incorrectly. I hurried back to the boys' room, applied the second Band-Aid to the six-year-old's knee as quickly as I could, and turned to leave, intent on getting back to the piano bench, only to feel the four-year-old tug on my trouser leg. He gestured to me to put my ear next to his lips again.

Then he whispered that he wanted his mother. By then so did I.

Leaving Edita to tell the boys a story, I returned to the piano bench to listen, yet again, to the C-major scale. There are days when the only family value in our household is just hanging on.

Yet even on evenings like this one, I find raising children incomparably more satisfying than anything else I have ever done. When I was single all I thought about was myself. Would I get a good or bad speech assignment when the next batch of work was handed out? Would I get a good or bad seat assignment the next time I flew on Air Force One? Now all I think about is money. Yet there is nothing self-absorbed about it. I have mortgage payments to make, medical bills to pay, clothes to buy—I never understood how fleetingly time passes until I began watching four children outgrow their sneakers. Working to support my family is the least selfish way I have ever lived.

I keep thinking back to one of those passages on the Web site of the Texas GOP. "The traditional family and the values it fosters are the foundation of American society." When I read those words I can almost hear them being intoned by a sanctimonious southern voice, as if Jerry Falwell were giving a sermon in my head. But you know what? I believe them.

"Okay, here's the way it sorts out between me and the South," I said. David Brady, in his office at Stanford business school, where he is an associate dean, leaned back in his chair and put one foot up on his desk. David, I had learned, subscribed, at least in part, to the anti-southern school of thought. I wanted to have it out with him.

"I'm skeptical of the South," I continued. "I can't stand grits. I don't buy CDs by the Gatlin Brothers, and I would pay good money not to have to listen to Reba McEntire.

"But look at what has happened in American culture. Just half a century ago getting divorced was difficult, abortion was illegal, and the idea that two gays or lesbians should be granted the same legal status as a husband and wife would have been considered ridiculous. Half a century, David, that's all—half a century and the entire moral order has been turned upside down. Southern Republicans are just about the only people who have the courage to suggest that throwing out five thousand years of Judeo-Christian moral teaching might not be such a hot idea. Remember that quotation from Flannery O'Connor? 'You have to push as hard as the age that pushes against you.' Southern Republicans aren't letting themselves get pushed around—not by northern liberals, not by popular culture, not by the age. They're pushing back good and hard. And I say God bless 'em."

"You say 'God bless 'em?' " David replied. "I say the year is 1870. White southerners are watching their former slaves get elected to state legislatures. There's only one group of people that pushes back, and that's the Ku Klux Klan. So white people say, 'God bless *them.*' "

"Oh, come on," I replied. "The Klan was wrong and everybody knows it. What I'm arguing is that the moral values of southern Republicans are the moral values that shaped western culture."

"And what I'm arguing is that times change." David took his foot down from the desk. "Look," he continued, "I don't buy Caldwell's argument that the South is driving the rest of the country away from the GOP. The South these days is becoming more and more like everyplace else, and most Republicans in the South are like most Republicans outside the South. But where Caldwell has a point is with the religious right—the Jerry Falwells and the Pat Robertsons. If you've got a party in which people like that are setting the tone, then you can be sure the party won't carry the Northeast or California. Fortunately the tone these days is being set by George W. Bush, and he's a compassionate conservative, with the emphasis on 'compassionate,' not a moralizer."

"Not a moralizer? But, David, half the reason Bush has been doing so well in the polls is that people are sick of Clinton's immorality. Don't look so pained. 'Immorality' is a perfectly good word, even if the only place it gets used these days is south of the Mason-Dixon line."

David eyed me for a moment. "Are you saying you want to bring back the morality that I grew up with in the 1950s? Is that it? No sex before marriage? Gays forced to stay in the closet? Peter, let me clue you in, that world is gone. Restore the nuclear family? With mommy keeping house while daddy goes to work? We've got a divorce rate of 50 percent. More than half of all women work outside the home. Outlaw abortion? Something like 70 percent of the public wants abortion to be available in certain circumstances."

"So what are *you* saying?" I replied. "That there are no enduring moral values? That the sexual revolution was right but the Ten Commandments were all a big mistake?"

"I'm not talking values, I'm talking politics," David said. "And if the religious right tries to turn back the clock to the 1950s, it's going to make the job of centrists like Bush—people who actually stand a chance of winning elections in this country—a lot harder. There aren't that many evangelicals—probably no more than a third of all southern Republicans, even in Deep South states like Mississippi and South Carolina. They can't turn the whole country against the GOP. But they can cause trouble, especially since the press will always play them up. Remember, the press *wants* the Republican Party to look like a bunch of throwbacks."

"You may be right." I replied. "But I'm not sure I even care. I'll say it again. Southern Republicans have courage. Sometimes you have to take positions even if they don't win votes."

"That's what I like," David said. "Politics as the art of the *im*possible."

In a way David Brady and I were doing nothing more than discussing one of the basic principles you'd hear described in Political Science 101 in any university in the country. Every political party faces a perpetual dilemma. To win, it must make compromises. Yet to make winning worthwhile, it must resist compromises, standing instead on principles.

Republicans in Dixie are the kind of people who believe that abortion should be restricted while guns are made available, not the other way around. Yet if David is correct—and he reads polls all the time—that's not exactly a winning position on the coasts.

What's the GOP to do? Drop family values and set to work building a base outside the South? That would please those who subscribe to the anti-southern school of thought. Insist on family values, retaining the southern base while trusting that, eventually, other regions will come to respect the integrity of the GOP's positions? That would please me.

The most likely outcome is of course neither and both. As professors in Political Science 101 would attest, no successful party will ever cut itself off from its base—or ever stop trying to expand it. Hence the dilemma—principles or compromises—is one the GOP can never escape, any more than Republicans in the East or West can ever escape their fellow Republicans down South.

Chapter Four

COOL AND UNCOOL, OR MEDIALAND

Journal entry:

On the Bush campaign jet from Los Angeles to Sacramento this morning, I sat with the press in coach while Bush and his staff sat up front, in first class. Once the jet reached cruising altitude, Bush's press secretary, Karen Hughes, a tall, broad-shouldered, businesslike woman, appeared from behind the curtain that separated the two compartments to walk down the aisle and talk with the press. I had been looking forward to meeting her. When she and I had spoken by telephone a couple of weeks before, Hughes could hardly have been friendlier. She had told me that although the governor wouldn't be giving any interviews during his swing through California, he might make an exception for me since I used to work for his father. Now, I thought, Hughes would recognize me, then find a quarter of an hour for me on the governor's schedule later today or tomorrow—for that matter, she might even take me forward to first class right now.

"How ya doin'?" Hughes asked, shaking my hand. Her voice was warm, but the look in her eyes was flat and official. I told her my name twice. Both times she replied simply, "Good to meet ya." When I tried to explain who I was,

Hughes turned away. She continued down the aisle, greeting reporters the same way she had greeted me, her voice friendly, her eyes keeping their distance. She reminded me of the treatment that American diplomats used to give their Soviet counterparts.

What had changed? When Hughes and I had spoken on the telephone, I realized, I had been a fellow Republican. Now I was a member of the media. As soon as I hung the press credentials around my neck, I might as well have defected.

Yes, I know. It seems odd for a book about Republicans to devote a chapter to the press and Hollywood, which are dominated by Democrats. But you cannot understand Republicans without understanding how much the news and entertainment media irk them. The GOP may have held the White House for half the postwar period and controlled both houses of Congress for the last six years, but resentment of the media remains as basic to the identity of Republicans as does resentment of the English to the identity of the Irish.

By traveling from the most Republican region of the country, Dixie, to the least Republican, the region inhabited, as it were, by the media, I hoped to benefit from the contrast. I understood why the South, once solidly Democratic, became Republican. Why couldn't the media do the same?

PLEASE LIKE US

The Republican attitude toward the press is easy enough to demonstrate. All you have to do is talk to a Republican. Shortly after he left office, Pete Wilson, the Republican governor of California, and I had breakfast together. My notes indicate that it took no more than eight sentences for Pete— he insisted I call him by his first name—to begin railing against the press. As governor, Pete supported Proposition 187, the 1994 ballot initiative under which the state of California would have denied all but emergency services to illegal immigrants. (The measure passed by large margins but was set aside in 1999 as the result of arbitration.) Pete told me that he had supported Proposition 187 on strict grounds. The federal government, which had failed in its duty to control the state's border with Mexico, had no right to force the state's taxpayers to provide illegal immigrants with the $3 to $4 billion in health care, education, and other services that they used each year. Yet the press had twisted Pete's position, making it seem racist. Pete shook his head in exasperation. "It's the goddamdest thing I've ever seen."

There you have the authentic voice of the Republican. Pete Wilson's political career spanned three decades. He served as a member of the California Assembly, as mayor of San Diego, as a United States senator, and as governor of the most populous state in the union, never losing a general election. What came to mind when he reflected upon his long and distinguished life in public service? Those sons of bitches in the press.

The governor had a point. Every poll of the press produces the same result. By a wide margin, the press is liberal. This bears repeating. The liberal press is no mere chimera of the Republican imagination. It exists. Consider just a few studies.

- In 1988 a newsletter called *The Journalist and Financial Reporting* surveyed 151 business reporters from more than thirty publications. The respondents were business reporters, mind you, the ones you'd expect to be as conservative as any reporters ever are. By an overwhelming majority, the reporters described themselves as "liberal."
- In 1989 the American Society of Newspaper Editors surveyed 1,200 reporters and editors at seventy-two newspapers. Those who identified themselves as "liberal" outnumbered those who identified themselves as "conservative" by three to one.
- In 1995 the Times Mirror Center for the People and the Press published a study that compared the attitudes of the press with those of the public. Among the public, 40 percent called themselves "conservative." Among the press? Five percent.
- In 1996 the Freedom Foundation and the Roper Center released a survey of 139 reporters and bureau chiefs in Washington, D.C. Four years earlier, in 1992, the study found, 89 percent of the reporters and bureau chiefs voted for Clinton, only 7 percent for Bush. The proportion who identified themselves as registered Democrats? Fifty percent. The proportion who identified themselves as registered Republicans? Four percent.

If you eavesdrop on Republicans when the subject of press bias comes up, first you'll hear them express their anger. But if you keep listening, eventually you'll hear them express something that sounds a lot like insecurity as well. Reporting, fact checking, analysis, writing—all the jobs that the press performs require considerable intelligence and skill. Republicans know that. If the press is composed of such bright, talented people, Republicans often wonder, and sometimes even ask out loud, then why don't they like us?

After years of trying to figure out why the press is biased against Republicans, I've collected just three explanations. Each contains some truth. Yet each suffers from limitations.

The first is that it's simply the nature of the press to be adversarial. As the old saw puts it, the job of a reporter is to "comfort the afflicted and afflict the comfortable." Since Republicans tend to be better off than Democrats—one of the most persistent patterns of American politics is that the higher a voter's position on the income distribution, the more likely he is to be a Republican—the press regards Republicans with suspicion.

The problem with this explanation? The new economy. There are now well-established high-tech and entertainment plutocracies, large groups of very, very rich people who tend to be Democratic, not Republican. But the press doesn't exactly line up to take them on.

The second explanation is that the structure of the news industry reflects the larger class structure of America itself. Reporters and editors get pushed around by Republican publishers, so they develop an antagonism for Republican bosses in society at large.

The trouble here? The explanation is decades out of date. Nowadays publishers are at least as liberal as their news staffs. Katherine Graham when she ran the *Washington Post*,

Otis Chandler when he was still at the *Los Angeles Times*, the Sulzbergers at the *New York Times*. As David Brady put it, "These people aren't Republican oppressors. They're liberal saints, for Pete's sake."

The third explanation is that Republicans make for bad copy. This explanation has always struck me as the most compelling. The Republican agenda, after all, is often quite negative. Smaller government, fewer programs, lower taxes. If a Republican like me had his way, the three-ring, Barnum & Bailey-sized federal government would be reduced to the scope of a flea circus. But what would the press write about then?

In 1992, just a few weeks before President Clinton took office, I had lunch with a friend who writes for the *New York Times*. He could hardly wait for the Bush administration to end. As he saw it, nearly all that Bush had done was give boring speeches, hold press conferences in which he mangled the language, and produce budgets in which he did nothing more inspired than split his differences with the Democrats. Clinton promised instead to give stirring speeches, hold quotable press conferences, and undertake dozens of dramatic policy initiatives. You might think my friend was talking like a liberal. He wasn't. He was talking like a reporter. What he saw was a simple set of truths. Bush equals bad copy, Clinton equals good copy.

The problem with this explanation? Ronald Reagan. Reagan equaled good copy—for most of the 1980s he equaled better copy than almost anyone else on the planet. He cut taxes, rebuilt the military, and held a series of summit meetings with Gorbachev, providing the press with one huge story after another. But I'd be willing to wager that even fewer members of the Washington press corps voted for Reagan than voted for Bush.

It's worth noting that the press is liberal in every western democracy in the world. "Look," David Brady told me, "the reason the press is liberal is one of those deep questions that combines history, psychology, and for all I know anthropology and half a dozen other disciplines. Why are WASPs Republicans?" David asked. "Why are the Irish Democrats? Who the hell knows? Sure, you can come up with this or that explanation, but none of them even comes close to a complete answer. You just have to take it as one of the stipulations of Democratic politics. The press is liberal. It just frigging well is."

Hence the Republican predicament. They'd like the press to like them—they really would. But it doesn't—and no matter how hard they try, Republicans can't quite figure out why.

SHOW ME THE MONEY

If you want a rough measure of the extent to which Hollywood is Democratic, look at political fund-raisers. President Clinton has held more than a dozen fund-raisers in Hollywood and its environs. The price per plate at these events has ranged from $5,000 to $10,000. Virtually every studio head, actor, agent, and supermodel of any standing has ponied up to attend at least one. Moguls such as Michael Eisner, David Geffen, Lew Wasserman, David Bronfman, and Steven Spielberg (Spielberg is so close to Clinton that Clinton has been an overnight guest in Spielberg's home). Stars such as Harrison Ford, Michelle Pfeiffer, Tom Cruise, Nicole Kidman, and Barbra Streisand (Streisand is so close to Clinton that she has stayed as an overnight guest in Clinton's home, the White House).

Now look at the Hollywood fund-raiser that Republican presidential contender George W. Bush held in June 1999. The price per plate was only $1,000. Even at that the only celebrities who turned up were Gary Collins, Bo Derek, Pat Boone, Robert Stack, and Warren Beatty. The first four aren't exactly on the Hollywood A-list, while the last, Warren Beatty, so surprised everyone by attending that at a press conference the next morning a reporter asked Bush what Beatty had been doing there. Obviously puzzled about it himself, Bush was able to offer only a joke: "I think he's secretly in love with my mother." A couple of weeks later it emerged that Beatty was considering a presidential run of his own. That explained it. When Republicans throw a Hollywood fund-raiser, the only big star who shows up is just there to take notes on how it's done.

Trying to figure out why the press is so liberal, you'll recall, I had several explanations to offer. Yet when I tried to figure out why Hollywood is so liberal, I was unable to offer any explanations at all. Neither could David Brady.

"You know that chain of restaurants, Planet Hollywood?" David said. "I've always liked the name. You know why? Because that's just what Hollywood is, a different planet."

While people like David and me understand the activities of the press in at least a rudimentary way—like the press, we spend a lot of our own time doing research and writing—the activities of actors, producers, and screenwriters lie entirely outside our field of experience. They might as well live on a different planet, just as David said.

"If you want to do something useful in the book of yours,"

David suggested, "go figure out Hollywood politics for your-self." I tried to do just that.

Since members of a minority are often the most acute observers of the majority, I decided to learn about Holly-wood Democrats by talking to Hollywood Republicans. I thought I'd start with the stars. This plan offered the ad-vantage of instantly narrowing my prospects. After years of hanging around Republican politics, I could name only three stars I felt reasonably certain were members of the GOP: Tom Selleck, Arnold Schwarzenegger, and Charlton Heston (Bruce Willis and Kevin Costner used to turn up for events at the Bush White House from time to time, but friends in the Bush administration told me that they did so out of loy-alty to the Bushes, not to the GOP). I called all three. All three stiffed me. Tom Selleck's publicist put me off by say-ing that Selleck was an Independent, not a Republican. Schwarzenegger's publicist put me off by the still more di-rect device of refusing to return any of my calls. Heston's publicist assured me that his client would get in touch with me as soon as he returned from Spain, where he was shoot-ing a movie. I'm still waiting. I might as well have been in Moscow during the old days, trying to get the stars of the Bolshoi to attack the Politburo on the record. When the stars refused to speak to me, I had no choice. I was forced to turn to dissidents.

During his two decades in Hollywood, Michael Medved became a film critic (for a time he was the co-host of the television program, *Sneak Previews*), then a critic of Holly-wood itself, attacking the entertainment industry in a num-ber of books, perhaps the best known of which is *Hollywood vs. America: Popular Culture and the War Against Tradi-*

tional Values. Eventually Medved got sick of Southern California and did what many Californians who get sick of Southern California do, moving north to Seattle. Now he hosts a nationally syndicated radio talk show. An intense, energetic man with tousled brown hair, large brown eyes, and a drooping handlebar mustache, Medved talked to me in his studio after one of his broadcasts. He offered two explanations for why Hollywood is so Democratic. Medved's first explanation: In Hollywood, emotion is more important than reason.

"In the entertainment industry, you have to have your emotions constantly available to you," Medved said. "You go to the set in the morning and meet some snot-nosed kid who makes it clear that he doesn't especially want to work with you. Then you have to spend all day crying because the script calls for the kid to have cancer. People in Hollywood spend their careers engaged in emotional self-manipulation, and a town that operates on emotional self-manipulation will lean to the left."

The Democratic and Republican positions on welfare, for example, illustrate Medved's point. Democrats say the government should spend more to help the poor. The emotional appeal of that position is immediate. It feels good. Republicans say, Not so fast. To spend more, Republicans argue, the government would have to raise taxes. That in turn would have a dampening effect on the economy. Can we be sure, Republicans ask, that the government wouldn't push as many people into poverty as it intended to help? When government money reached the poor, Republicans go on to ask, would it truly help them? Or would it demoralize them, making them dependent on the government? Instead of increasing government handouts, Republicans conclude, it would be better to fashion programs, like the welfare reform of 1996,[*] that help the poor get jobs, enabling them to care for their families on their own. The Republican position thus involves a thought process of three or four steps. And the thought process is made up of just that, thought. In a town that would rather emote than think, the Republican position doesn't stand a chance.

Medved's other explanation: sex. "The chief motivation for anyone in Hollywood," he said, "is getting laid."

Hollywood takes its morals from the marketplace. Competitive pressures are such that if one studio shows ankle, another will show leg, and another will show—well, you can see how one thing leads to another. For years the industry found itself subjected to censorship. The old Hays Office reviewed films before they were released, while censors working for the networks decided what could and could not be portrayed on television. Now such censorship has all but disappeared. Movies may portray whatever they want, subject only to a loose rating system. On television, prime-time programming has become much more sexually explicit than even after-hours programming of just a decade ago. (Watching *Ally McBeal* recently, I kept count. The word "penis" was used three times. Sexual intercourse was portrayed at least two times. I say "at least" because the way the bodies were positioned, it was hard to tell.)

What takes place on the set tends to take place in private life. Hollywood may never have been a paragon of virtue.

---

[*]Since the federal government enacted the welfare reform of 1996, welfare rolls across the country have dropped 40 percent. Although Democrats now associate themselves with the reform, the measure has a telling history. The Republican-controlled Congress passed the measure three times before President Clinton finally signed it.

But it used to observe certain standards. In the old days even the biggest stars had to sign contracts that contained clauses prohibiting "moral turpitude." If the stars misbehaved, they risked losing their jobs. Today? It is difficult to imagine an act that anyone in Hollywood would construe as misbehavior. Rob Lowe was sued for having sex with a minor, in an encounter captured on videotape. Lowe's career continues to flourish. Hugh Grant was arrested with a prostitute. Grant remains a major star. Since Hollywood has rejected traditional moral values, it has little time for the party of traditional moral values, the GOP.

"Everybody wants to date a supermodel," Medved said. "And if you want to succeed with really great-looking women, you'll have far more success if you're a member of the left than if you're a member of the right." In Hollywood, the pleasures of being a Democrat are, so to speak, too great to forgo.

Journal entry:

Waiting for Rob Long to arrive for breakfast this morning, I made notes on the scene around me. Everyone in the dining room of the Four Seasons Hotel in Beverly Hills wore clothes that looked simultaneously informal and exquisitely expensive. Everyone had a tan. Everyone had perfect teeth.

Two men and a woman sat at a table next to mine. The men wore black trousers and black three-button jackets over black shirts. The woman wore a black dress. The dress was cut low. It would have revealed her cleavage, if she had had any. Both men and the woman had hair that stuck straight up in little spikes and wore glasses with gun-

metal wire rims and tiny lenses. Eavesdropping as they lin-
gered over their juice—each had ordered only a single glass
of grapefruit juice—I actually overheard them using the
terms "red-lighted" and "green-lighted," as in, The studio
"red-lighted" my last project but has "green-lighted" my
next one.

Two thoughts crossed my mind. The first was that the
people in this dining room were the real thing, people liv-
ing the Hollywood dream. The second was that I was the
only Republican present.

Rob Long graduated from Yale in 1987, returned to his
prep school, Andover, to teach English for a year, got bored,
then left for Hollywood. A gifted writer—he had written a
number of student productions as an undergraduate—Long
enrolled in the writing program at the UCLA film school. "If
you were a writer," Long told me over breakfast, "film school
was really easy. I had one class a week, and I spent the rest
of the time on the beach."

During Long's first year in Hollywood, he became a conservative.

"A friend gave me a copy of *Modern Times*," Long explained. *Modern Times* is the history of the twentieth century
by the conservative English journalist Paul Johnson. When
he read the book, Long's own political thinking crystallized.
"Sitting on the beach in Santa Monica," Long said, "I kept
reading one thing after another that they'd never taught me
at Andover or Yale. I'd read something, and I'd say, 'Wait a
minute. I took advanced placement history. How come I never
knew *that*?' I'll give you an example. Remember the over-

throw of Allende in Chile? I was taught to believe that it was all a plot by Richard Nixon and American corporations. Then in *Modern Times* I read that under Allende the inflation in Chile got up to 6,000 percent. I said, 'Whoa. That probably had a *lot* more to do with the overthrow of Allende than Richard Nixon or American corporations *ever* did.' "

When he wasn't lying on the beach reading *Modern Times* or attending UCLA, Long worked on scripts with his friend Dan Staley, who had graduated from Yale two years ahead of him. When, in less than a year, their scripts impressed the right people, Long and Staley were hired to produce the final three seasons of one of the most popular and profitable situation comedies in the history of television, *Cheers*. Long and Staley were, respectively, 24 and 26.

Long has remained a figure in the television business ever since, helping, as half of Staley/Long Productions, to produce a string of situation comedies—when we met, he was casting for *Love and Money*, to be aired on CBS. Long has also remained a conservative, writing regularly for *National Review* magazine, an activity that his friends in Hollywood pass off as an eccentric hobby, like raising bonsai trees or mastering French cooking. Still in his thirties, Long looks even younger, partly because he has a round, cherubic face, partly because his success as a producer permits him to dress precisely as he chooses, ignoring Hollywood chic to attire himself as if he were still at Yale, wearing wrinkled khakis and wrinkled dress shirts, his hair combed, not spiked. Why was Hollywood so Democratic? "First I'll tell you about a couple of things that other people would tell you about," Long said. "Then I'll tell you what I think myself."

The first thing other people would tell me about was the blacklist. "What you'll hear over and over in this town is that it was the blacklist that made Hollywood liberal," Long said. The blacklist arose during the McCarthy era, when the studios shut out, or blacklisted, members of the entertainment industry who were alleged to have Communist sympathies, most famously a group of producers, directors, and writers who came to be known as "The Hollywood Ten." "Since the blacklist was an instrument of the right," Long continued, "it proved that the right is hostile to the creative community. At least that's the theory."

It was a theory about which Long had his doubts. The usual view of the blacklist is that it constituted an act of gross unfairness, mangling the careers of innocent people. Yet materials from the Russian archives make it clear that there were indeed Communist cells in Hollywood. The right may have engaged in red-baiting, but the left provided plenty of reds to bait. Anyway, it is difficult to see why events of half a century ago, when many of those running the entertainment industry hadn't even been born, should dominate the politics of Hollywood today.

The second thing other people would tell me about was Hollywood's Jewishness. It was widely believed, although for reasons of political correctness seldom stated, that Hollywood was Democratic because it was Jewish. The tycoons who built Hollywood were indeed Jewish—Harry Cohn, Samuel Goldwyn, Louis B. Mayer, Jack and Harry Warner—and the town has remained disproportionately Jewish ever since. Ever since the New Deal, in turn, Jews have been overwhelmingly Democratic. "Take a guy like Michael Eisner [the Jewish chairman of Disney]," Long said. "A Republican could cut his taxes, deregulate every business that he's in, and promise to protect Israel. He'd say, 'Thank you very much.' Then he'd go right out and vote Democratic."

Yet although Jews, who make up about 3 percent of the population of the country, may make up as much as 15, 20, or perhaps even 30 percent of the population of the entertainment industry, Hollywood still has a large gentile majority. If gentiles in Hollywood voted the way gentiles in Kansas vote, Hollywood would be predominantly Republican despite the large Jewish population. Instead the gentiles vote just as overwhelmingly Democratic as do the Jews.

Now that he had dispensed with the opinions of other people, Long offered me his own. "You want to know what I think is the real explanation?" he asked. "Money." Long believed that Hollywood was Democratic because it was full of people who had done just what he himself had done, breezing into town to discover that they could make large sums of money with almost laughable ease.

"It's not that people out here don't work hard," Long said. "They do. They put in long hours under a lot of pressure. But writing scripts or acting don't feel like work in the same way that going down coal mines or teaching first graders or harvesting crops feel like work." Because their money comes to them so easily, people in Hollywood tend to demonstrate the same traits that people who inherit their wealth tend to demonstrate. Feeling guilty about having so much, they attempt to absolve themselves by performing good works. They give to charities. They join museum committees. And they support Democrats.

"What does it cost them?" Long said. "So they support higher taxes that working people will have to make sacrifices to pay. So what? People in Hollywood will be among the richest people in the country no matter how high taxes go. So they support bilingual education and it holds Hispanic kids back instead of helping them get ahead. So what? The people in this town would never *dream* of sending their kids to public schools. Never. People here get to take any political position they want because they know that they'll never have to deal with the consequences of those positions in their own lives. They're reflexively left-wing because their money frees them from any accountability."

By way of example, Long explained the economics of his current project, *Love and Money*. He and his partner had hired more than half a dozen writers. The lowest paid would receive a salary of several hundred thousand dollars. After having breakfast with me, Long would join his partner to begin casting the show. Actors in even the smallest roles would receive salaries, again, of several hundred thousand dollars. If the show succeeded, everyone involved in the project would make even more money. If at the end of a run of several years the show was sold into syndication—in other words if stations bought *Love and Money* to show the reruns—everyone would make more money still, with Long and his partner, who would receive 30 percent of the proceeds, standing to make many millions of dollars.

Long glanced at his watch. "Gotta run," he said. I made no effort to delay him. There was too much money at stake.

Journal entry:

Rob Long had a bowl of cornflakes and a glass of orange juice. I had a muffin, a glass of orange juice, and a cup of coffee. With the tip, the bill came to $52. There must be just as much money in this town as Long claims, or even the Four Seasons wouldn't have had the nerve.

After breakfast with Rob Long, I drove to a studio in a converted warehouse on a far edge of Los Angeles to see Michael Beugg, a friend with whom I attended business school. Unlike Rob Long and Michael Medved, Mike isn't a dissident from liberal Hollywood—for that matter, Mike isn't even a Republican—and I stopped by just to say hello, not to talk politics. But when Mike, a line producer, heard why I was in town, he promptly added another reason why Hollywood is Democratic. "Isn't it obvious?" Mike said. "This is a union town."

The relationship between unions and the Democratic Party is an old one. As far back as the first years of the republic, urban workers sided with the Democratic-Republicans, the precursors of the Democrats, while opposing the Federalists, the precursors of the Republicans. Early in this century the Democratic Party, notably under Alfred E. Smith, governor of New York, championed the growth of unions, and then at mid-century the Democratic Party, under President Franklin Roosevelt, made organized labor one of the central components of the New Deal coalition. The relationship between unions and the Democratic Party has sometimes proven uneasy—when George McGovern received the Democratic presidential nomination in 1972, George Meany, chairman of the AFL-CIO and a hawk on Vietnam, refused to permit his union to endorse McGovern—but the Democratic Party has always remained the natural home for organized labor all the same.

Here in Hollywood, Mike explained, the people who run the studios and production companies hire and fire at will— he had only gotten his current position because the two line producers who preceded him had both been dismissed after only a couple of weeks on the job. And since there were always more people who wanted to work in the entertainment industry than there were jobs, individual workers found themselves in an impossibly weak bargaining position. The transitory nature of the work compounded their insecurity. When a soundman or makeup artist was on a project, it was difficult to predict how long the project would last. When he was between projects, it was difficult to say how long the layoff would last.

"People here depend on their unions," Mike said. Hollywood workers saw unions as a way of making certain they received benefits, such as health insurance, and wages high enough to enable them to survive from one project to the next. While Rob Long had told me what life was like for people at the top of the Hollywood pay structure, Mike Beugg was telling me what life was like for everybody else. "When you're watching the Academy Awards or the Emmys, you're only seeing the people at the very top of the business. There are thousands of others who work in this town," he explained. Hollywood gave most of them neither fame nor riches, just a precarious way of making a living.

To illustrate this point, Mike took me to watch a scene being filmed. The scene was one of dozens in the made-for-TV movie that the company with which Mike was working, Imani Pictures, was shooting for BET, Black Entertainment Television. The scene involved only two actors, yet the set was jammed with more than 60 people. I wasn't able to take notes fast enough to keep up with him as Mike, whispering, identified all the people, but those present included the director, the first assistant director, the second assistant director, the executive producer, the supervising producer, three or four production assistants, the script supervisor, the director of photography, several camera assistants, three electricians, a gaffer, several grips, a sound mixer, a boom man, a prop master, an assistant prop master, a wardrobe supervisor, and three or four makeup artists and hairdressers. Every one of them belonged to a union.

Back in his office, Mike explained that he himself had had to join the Directors Guild of America, and that he now acted as the liaison between the production company and half a dozen unions, including the Screen Actors Guild, the Writers Guild, and the Directors Guild. "Hollywood may be full of thin, articulate, beautiful people," Mike said. "But unions are just as important to folks in this town as they are to the big burly guys who work in factories in Detroit."

Mike's telephone rang. After he picked it up, Mike covered the mouthpiece. "Sorry. I have to take this one. It's Joe over at the Teamsters."

Union membership, easy money, and lots of sex. I'm not sure those add up to a complete explanation of why Hollywood is Democratic, but they certainly set Hollywood apart from any Republican town that comes to mind.

Every so often French intellectuals denounce American films and television programs, claiming that Hollywood is undermining their culture. It is hard to imagine that Republicans have much in common with people who chain-smoke Gitanes cigarettes and read Camus, but members of the GOP know how the French intellectuals feel. Sex, violence, foul language, mocking portrayals of figures, such as businessmen or clergy, that Republicans respect—all of it can seem as much of an intrusion to members of the GOP in Kansas or Alabama as depictions of the Wild West must seem to intellectuals in Paris.

What do Republicans intend to do about Hollywood? What *can* they do? Whenever a Bob Dole or a Dan Quayle attacks

Hollywood, he looks stuffy and old-fashioned, even to Republicans themselves. Hollywood is cool. Republicans are uncool. Some in the GOP believe that new technologies will eventually loosen Hollywood's grip on popular culture. The recent movie *The Blair Witch Project* was produced outside Hollywood for less than one hundred thousand dollars. When it became a hit, I got a flurry of e-mails from Republicans, gleefully advancing the theory that a decade or two from now Hollywood will find itself forced to compete with studios throughout the heartland. Perhaps. In the meantime just about all Republicans can do is watch reruns of *The Andy Griffith Show* and *The Brady Bunch*, nurturing memories of an earlier time, like the Irish singing old ballads during the English occupation.

THE EXPERIMENT

As much as Hollywood irks them, when Republicans complain about the media, what they keep coming back to is the press.

Tony Dolan, President Reagan's chief speechwriter and the author of the phrase "evil empire," always told the speechwriters in the Reagan White House not to worry about the press. "If the American people really believed all they read in the newspapers," Tony would say, "the country would be Communist by now." What Tony was talking about, of course, was the long term, the period over which the good judgment and common sense of the American people will always prevail. You can't fool all of the people all of the time. The trouble is, that still leaves the short term. This is the period over which even Tony worried about the press. As above the fray as Tony liked to appear, if you had walked into his office one evening after the president had given a speech, you would have seen Tony scrambling to get into the fray. He would have been on the telephone, dialing again and again to get through to Lou Cannon of the *Washington Post* and Jerry Boyd of the *New York Times* before their deadlines. When he reached them, Tony would have pleaded, wheedled, cajoled, and begged—anything to dissuade them from reporting the president's remarks in a negative light. You can fool all of the people some of the time, and Republicans are convinced that whenever it can, the press does just that.

Of course Republicans are seldom able to prove this proposition. How could they? Would the election of 1992 have been different if the press had reported on the economic recovery when it began, midway through the year, instead of continuing to report on factory closings and unemployed workers even after the recession had ended? Would George Bush have been reelected president? Would the GOP have picked up seats in Congress? Republicans think so. They think they *know* so. But they are hardly able to experiment with history, holding other elements of the campaign constant while they change the press.

Every so often, however, history provides an experiment of its own. Consider the 1984 vice presidential debate between George Bush and Geraldine Ferraro.

I helped prepare Bush for the encounter, sitting in on the mock debates that were held to give him some practice. The mock debates took place in the third-floor auditorium of the Old Executive Office Building, the ornate granite structure across West Executive Avenue from the White House itself. Bush stood behind a lectern on one side of the stage while Lynn Martin stood behind a lectern on the other. A Re-

publican member of Congress and a friend of Bush's, Lynn
Martin impersonated Geraldine Ferraro. It proved a tough assignment. Not that Martin lacked the talent. She was at least
as combative and funny as Ferraro herself. But the vice president had no idea how to confront a woman. First he would
prove gentlemanly to the point of passivity, as if the code of
chivalry required him to lose the debate. Then he would shift
to the attack, appearing, well, ungentlemanly. When Bush was
passive, Martin had to goad him. When he grew aggressive,
she had to scold him, telling him to settle down. Goad, scold.
Throughout the mock debates Martin kept at it, striving to
even out the vice president's performance.

It worked. At least I thought it worked. So did most
Americans—at first. And this is my point. Polls taken immediately after the debate showed that George Bush had
trounced Geraldine Ferraro—one survey declared Bush the
victor by 19 percent.

Then the press went to work. It harped on a single exchange. Suggesting that Reagan was no tougher on terrorists
than Carter had been, Ferraro had compared the 1983 bombing of our embassy in Lebanon with the 1979 taking of
hostages in Iran. Replying, Bush had attempted to draw a distinction between the two incidents, beginning his answer, "Let
me help you with the difference, Mrs. Ferraro, between Iran
and the embassy in Lebanon." Ferraro had grown indignant,
accusing Bush of patronizing her. The television commenta-
tors replayed the exchange again and again, describing the
vice president's demeanor toward Ferraro as if he had been
a Viking and she a nun. Within an hour the polls began to
change. Bush's margin of victory narrowed. A poll on *Night-
line* showed that Bush had won by only 9 percent. Later polls
showed Bush's margin of victory shrinking still more. By the

following morning, the *Washington Post* was able to report no clear winner.

As a demonstration of the effect the press has on voters, the incident could hardly have been neater if it had been designed in a laboratory. When they saw the debate for themselves, Americans reached one conclusion. When they saw the debate through the medium of the press, they reached a different conclusion. It was, to use Pete Wilson's phrase, the goddamdest thing.*

Pondering the relationship between Republicans and the press, I reached two conclusions. The first is that campaign finance reform will never be enacted as long as Republicans can stop it. The second is that even though as I write Senator John McCain is leading in the contest for the Michigan primary, McCain is unlikely to grasp the Republican presidential nomination. Permit me to explain.

FLAK

As we have seen, Republicans are convinced that the press skews the political contest against them. Consider, for example, John Morgan, the friend who used to work across the

---

*The 1991 Supreme Court confirmation hearings for Clarence Thomas amount to another neat demonstration of the effect the press has on voters. During the hearings, you'll recall, Anita Hill, who once worked for Clarence Thomas at the Equal Employment Opportunity Commission, charged that Thomas had subjected her to sexual harassment. Thomas denied the charges. Polls showed that a majority of the public believed Thomas, not Hill. In the months that followed, the press treated Thomas skeptically and Hill as an injured heroine. The polls began to shift. One year later, polls showed that a majority of the public believed Hill, not Thomas.

hall from me when I was writing speeches for Vice President Bush. John is now a political consultant. Although the GOP has the support of the great mass of ordinary Americans, John believes, the press remains a serious tactical problem. "We're like a vast army," John says. "But we have no air coverage because we don't control the media. The media comes over and sweeps down like dive-bombers, and it scatters us."

What flak can Republicans put in the air to combat the media dive-bombers? The answer is simple. Advertising. "If we as Republicans don't get our message delivered properly through the national media," Congressman Christopher Cox of California told me, "then we have to make up for that fact with paid advertising." Republicans believe they have no choice. They must resort to selling themselves the way Coke sells soft drinks or Procter & Gamble sells soap. Former Speaker of the House Newt Gingrich put it this way: "Republicans are on defense for one year and ten-and-a-half months out of every two-year cycle. It's only when you go to paid advertising in the last six weeks [of campaign season] that Republicans are able to be on offense."

There's just one problem with paid advertising. You have to pay for it. In every election cycle, Republicans thus find themselves in need of a great deal of money. Under the current regime of election laws, they're able to raise it. But under the reforms now being proposed, they wouldn't. So? So Republicans block the reforms. There is a second and nobler reason for opposing the reforms than the damage they would do to Republican electoral prospects: As the Supreme Court has held, political money is essential to political speech, so the reforms would pose a direct threat to the First Amendment. Republican officeholders do make this argument. They make it every time they vote to block or water down another campaign finance reform. But even as they're talking about free speech, it is easy to suspect, they're thinking about all the money they still need to raise before election day.

The exception, of course, is presidential candidate Senator John McCain of Arizona. McCain, as everyone knows, is ardent in the cause of campaign finance reform. He has said that "all of us have been corrupted by the process . . . where big money has bought access which has bought influence." No doubt McCain believes this assertion. But he cannot adduce any evidence to support it. In study after study, political scientists have found that officeholders vote according to two factors, the views they themselves hold and the views their constituents hold. The sources of their campaign money play no demonstrable role. Perhaps the most famous studies are those that examine the voting patterns of senators and representatives after they announce their intention to retire. No longer in need of campaign money, these officeholders suddenly find themselves in the position of congressional monks, owing allegiance to no one but their maker. Yet none changes his voting patterns. Either the officeholders in these studies go on voting to please special interests for the fun of it, an obviously dubious proposition, or they were never voting to please special interests in the first place. Politicians don't go looking for contributors to whom they can sell themselves. Contributors go looking for politicians who already hold views they find amenable. Policy comes first. The money follows.

Since Senator McCain's home state of Arizona is one of the few places in the country in which the press lacks the usual liberal bias—to this day, for example, the *Arizona Republic*, once owned by Dan Quayle's grandfather, Eugene Pulliam, remains moderate to conservative—John McCain might find that he could win elections just as easily after the passage of campaign finance reform as before. Very few other Republicans would fare as well. "I like John," Pete Wilson said to me about McCain. "But his reform would destroy our party."

He will be hard-pressed to win the support of a party in which so many officeholders and activists see him as a threat. I grant that he might prove me wrong. But if he does, study the faces of the delegates to the GOP convention when McCain delivers his acceptance speech. Behind their smiles, many of them will be grinding their teeth.

Journal entry:

Today I received a letter from former President Bush.

I had written him to check my memory of the 1984 vice presidential debate. After making it clear that our memories match—"I think we clearly won that debate . . . but the spinmeisters went to work"—Bush added a postscript. It describes an incident that had always puzzled me.

The incident took place the day after the debate. Bush visited the New Jersey docks to shake hands with longshoremen. While there, he said of his encounter with Ferraro that he "kicked a little ass." The press presented his remark as another instance of Bush's hopelessly patronizing attitude toward women. It created a furor. Watching the evening news back in Washington, I had been perplexed. The remark sounded so out of character. In public Bush was always as prim in his use of language as the dean of an Episcopal prep school. What had gotten into him?

"One of the longshoremen," Bush explained in his let-

ter, "showed his support by holding up a sign. The sign said 'You Kicked Ass.' Yes, that patriot followed me all around the dock, his self-written sign proudly displayed whenever a TV camera came into view. As I climbed into my VP limo at the end of the visit to the docks, I did say to him quietly, 'Yes, we did kick a little ass.' I had not seen the boom mike held over my shoulder. The national press went crazy—as if none of them had ever heard such a pithy sporting expression before."

I should have known. An ambush. By the press.

Chapter Five

CONVERTS

Journal entry:

Flying back to California after visiting my brother in Seattle, I closed my eyes and tried to imagine what it would be like. "Don," I saw myself saying, "I have something important to tell you. After years of wrestling with the issues, I've decided to become a Democrat." My brother responded with a long silence. Then he started laughing.

That was wrong. My brother wouldn't see anything funny about it. I tried imagining the scene a different way. "Don," I saw myself saying this time, "I've done something, and I don't want you to try to talk me out of it. I've become a Democrat."

My brother responded with the same long silence. Then he got angry. "How could you do that? How could you turn your back on the family?"

That wasn't any better. My brother would know that getting angry would only make me stubborn. I tried imagining the scene yet a different way.

"Don," I said, "I know this may come as something of a shock to you, but I've decided to become a Democrat." My brother responded with a long silence. Then . . .

It was no use. I couldn't devise a scene that proved coherent. Me? Become a Democrat? It was literally unimaginable.

At any given time, political scientists estimate, only about 20 percent of voters belong to a party other than the one in which they grew up. (For the purpose of these statistics, political scientists treat Independents as a party in their own right.) This figure implies that in any given election year—the time when most of those who change their party registration do so—only a tiny proportion of voters, perhaps as little as 3 or 4 percent, turn their backs on the party in which they were raised to join another party instead. Yet tiny as their numbers are, these voters prove crucial to both of the major parties. Now at rough parity—registered Democrats outnumber registered Republicans, but fewer Democrats vote, offsetting the Democratic advantage—the Republican and Democratic parties can each achieve the majority status it craves only by winning converts.

Working on this book, I thought for a moment that I could imagine what it would be like to leave the GOP to join the Democratic Party instead. It would be great. I'd be leaving the uncool for the cool, the dour and straitlaced for the free-spirited, the hard-hearted for the compassionate. Looking into the mirror as I shaved each morning, I'd say to myself, "You see that? That is the face of a man who *cares*." Then I recognized a problem. To keep members of my family from hearing about my switch secondhand, I'd have to tell them about it myself. As my journal entry indicates, I couldn't imagine doing so. I just couldn't.

That made me wonder. If I had been unable to imagine going from the GOP to the Democratic Party, what must it be like to go the other way? From cool to uncool, from free-spirited to dour and straitlaced, from compassionate to hardhearted? Why would anybody do it? Once you found a few who had, could they tell you anything the GOP could learn from?

I investigated the matter by talking to three converts I happened to know. I had never given their conversion to the Republican Party any thought. Now I saw that each had done something noteworthy, all the more so since each had grown up in an especially Democratic tribe. One was a Jew, one was an African-American, and one was a Catholic.

HAVE A FULFILLING SABBATH

As he conducts his radio show, a call-in show that reaches more than a hundred markets, Michael Medved sits at a table, a microphone in front of him, earphones on his head. His eyes remain in constant motion. He glances down at notes and newspaper clippings that lie strewn across the table, left to a computer screen that lists the topics that callers, waiting on hold, want to discuss, then up to a pane of glass, behind which stand his producers, to whom he signals with nods and hand gestures. One of Medved's legs jitters up and down, as if dispensing opinions for three hours a day represents an insufficient outlet for his energy. I sat in his booth with him for ninety minutes, just half of one of his broadcasts. In that time Medved took up more than a dozen topics.

He railed against the bombing of Serbia, which was then still taking place. By attacking Russia's historic ally, Medved argued, we were strengthening the hands of the anti-western faction in the Russian parliament. "Here we win this historic victory in the Cold War—thank you, President Reagan—here we win this historic victory over what was rightly called the 'evil empire,' and now we're in danger of bringing the Communists back to power." He aired a report on President Clinton's visit to Seattle earlier that afternoon, playing a chant that protesters shouted when Clinton was delayed: "He's late. He's late. He must have had a date." He attacked the Republicans in Congress, not from the left, but from the right, agreeing with a caller who thought the GOP was failing to stand up for itself. "You're right," Medved said. "The Republicans are behaving like a puppy that's been hit on the head with a newspaper." He reviewed two made-for-TV movies, *Joan of Arc* and *Noah's Ark*, and the new *Star Wars* movie, *The Phantom Menace,* attacking his fellow movie critics, who were all panning the *Star Wars* film, as "elitist." "There are so many *wonderful* characters in this thing," he proclaimed. "The film is *terrific*." Medved mocked the Canadian province of British Columbia, where the police had been handing out free cell phones to prostitutes, hoping for leads on a serial killer. "Those wacky Canadians. They've done it again." The police should be rounding the girls up, Medved argued, not giving them phones they could use to book more business. And he railed against Jesse Ventura's just-published autobiography, in which Ventura admitted that he didn't wear underwear. "I mean, do we really need to know this?"

As pugnacious a conservative as Rush Limbaugh, Medved nevertheless differs from Limbaugh in several regards. Whereas Limbaugh is grandiloquent, Medved prefers a light touch, engaging in conversations with his callers instead of lecturing them, and whereas Limbaugh sticks to politics, Medved comments regularly on popular culture, making book, television, and film reviews a staple of his show. But the most marked difference between the two probably lies in the way they deal with religion. Limbaugh ordinarily mentions religion only obliquely, seldom doing more than acknowledging his belief in traditional values. Medved talks about religion openly. When he reviewed *Joan of Arc*, for instance, Medved praised the respectful manner in which the movie portrayed Joan's faith. Medved's callers respond in kind, talking about religion just as openly as he does. Medved regularly receives calls from avowed Christians, the kind who know their Bible verses. The day I listened in, one of Medved's callers worried about Democratic moral standards. "How would I say it?" the caller said. "Democrats promote an immoral lifestyle." Another caller commented on the distribution of cell phones to prostitutes in British Columbia. "Scripture is real clear on this, Michael," the caller said. " 'Woe to a nation that calls 'evil' 'good' and 'good' 'evil.' ' " Even some of Medved's sponsors are Christian. Among ads for "Comfort Airbeds," AMICA Insurance, and Amazon.com, Medved ran an ad for Crosswalk.com, "the ultimate site for Christians on the Web."

There is something odd about Medved's being so conservative. There is something even odder about his eliciting so much of a response from evangelical Christians. Michael Medved is an Orthodox Jew. "Have a good weekend," Medved said, wrapping up the Friday show on which I sat in. "And have a fulfilling Sabbath, whenever you celebrate the Sabbath."

Jews are overwhelmingly Democratic. During the New Deal, they regularly cast about 85 percent of their votes for President Franklin Roosevelt. In more recent years, Jews cast roughly 80 percent of their votes for Presidents Kennedy and Johnson and for Senator Hubert Humphrey when he ran for president against Richard Nixon in 1968. In both 1992 and 1996, Jews cast about 78 percent of their votes for President

Clinton. Only African-Americans cast larger percentages of their votes for Democrats, and even then only by a few points.

It is easy enough to understand why Jews first became Democrats. Although the Jewish presence in America dates from colonial times—one synagogue in Rhode Island has been in use since 1763—by far the largest influx of Jews arrived in America between roughly 1880 and 1924, during the great wave of immigration that brought millions to this country from Eastern and Southern Europe. Like the Italians, Slavs, and others with whom they arrived, Jews were slow to become politically active—it took a while for immigrants who landed on Ellis Island to get the idea that this country belonged to them just as much as to the descendants of immigrants who landed on Plymouth Rock—and it was not until the 1930s that they got into the habit of voting. Still poor, they naturally gave their allegiance to the Democratic Party, the party of the little man.

The party of the little man. This requires a word of explanation. When the GOP was founded, it was the party of the little man itself. At least it thought so. As we have seen, it drew much of its support from one sort of little men, rural folk in the North, and it championed those who were, so to speak, the littlest men of all, the slaves. Yet after the Civil War the Republican Party began a long and close association with big business. It elicited the support of the men who were industrializing the nation—titans such as the railroad magnate Leland Stanford, benefactor of Stanford University, who served as the Republican governor of California and as a Republican member of the Senate. The Republican Party imposed tariffs on manufactured goods, helping to sustain the profits of these new industrialists while forcing ordinary Americans to pay more for products of all kinds. When Mrs.

Astor held her famous ball for the New York 400, she might as well have billed it as a gathering for the Republican Party's staunchest supporters.

There was one Republican, President Theodore Roosevelt, who stood up to business, reviving the nearly forgotten Sherman Anti-Trust Act to bring suit against dozens of corporations. But when William Howard Taft succeeded Roosevelt as president, Taft reverted to laissez-faire, and the Republican association with big business resumed.

During the 1920s the relationship between the GOP and business reached its apex. Business produced goods and services at a rate that raised the standard of living to levels theretofore unknown. Benefiting from the boom, the GOP held the White House and both houses of Congress for most of the decade. "The chief business of the American people," announced Calvin Coolidge, the man who as president led the Republican Party from 1923 to 1929, "is business." Then came the Great Depression.

After succeeding Calvin Coolidge in the White House, Herbert Hoover had the misfortune to be president when the Depression struck. The irony is that by Republican standards Hoover was something of a progressive. He believed in activist government. He used the Federal Farm Board to supply relief to farmers and the Reconstruction Finance Corporation to supply capital to the banking system. If he had been reelected in 1932, Hoover might have pursued some of the same policies as did the man to whom he lost, the Democrat Franklin Roosevelt. Yet none of this mattered. When Hoover gave speeches to restore public confidence, he seemed merely to be telling people to buck up and bear it. Encampments of the homeless, huddling in tents and sheds, soon became known as Hoovervilles.

By contrast, Franklin Roosevelt promised a New Deal, which, while lacking in specifics, at least sounded encouraging. Elected in 1932 in a landslide, Roosevelt spent the first years of his presidency enacting one piece of legislation after another intended to help labor, farmers, and the needy. The Depression never really ended until the Second World War, when the production of war matériel reopened the factories and created new jobs. But while economists now doubt that the New Deal played much of a role in the nation's economic recovery, there is no doubt that it played a role in the lives of the voters, giving them new hope. Thus did the Democratic Party, and emphatically not the Republican Party, become the party of the little man.

It is, as I say, easy enough to understand why Jews first became Democrats. It is a lot harder to understand why they are still Democrats. As immigrant groups become more affluent, they become more Republican. The Irish, Italians, Slavs, and every other immigrant group you can name have all conformed to this pattern. The only exception are the Jews. In the words of Seymour Martin Lipset, Jews today "live like Episcopalians but vote like Puerto Ricans." Why?

There seem to be two reasons. Marty Lipset himself emphasizes the Jewish fear of anti-Semitism. The descendants of people subjected to anti-Semitism for centuries, American Jews fear anti-Semitism even today. According to the 1999 Survey of American Jewish Opinion, American Jews name anti-Semitism as the greatest threat they face. "When you ask people which groups are more likely to be anti-Semitic," Marty says, "Jews answer Republicans and groups that support the Republicans, such as conservatives, businesspeople, and evangelical Christians." Jews remain loyal to the Democratic Party, therefore, because they see the GOP as their enemy.

The second reason Jews are Democratic is that Jews are liberal—the most liberal ethnic group in the country. To cite one statistic, Jews are more than twice as likely to be pro-choice as members of any other ethnic group. To cite another, Jews are four times more likely than the members of other ethnic groups to come right out and identify themselves as "liberal." Long after Democratic politicians have learned to avoid the l-word, Jews embrace it.

Dedicated liberals who see Republicans as anti-Semites. These are not likely GOP voters. So why did Michael Medved convert?

Slouching in a chair in a conference room after the show, Medved explained that there were three reasons why he left the Democratic Party to become a Republican. "First, I became more religious."

When in his late twenties he became an observant Jew, Medved said, his political outlook changed. He found himself drawn to the way the Republican Party stood up for traditional morality, which he now took seriously. At the same time, he found that he had stopped worrying about anti-Semitism among some of the GOP's most ardent supporters, evangelical Christians. "Evangelical Christians worry secular Jews," Medved said. "They don't upset the devout nearly as much. People of faith understand people of faith."

The second reason for Medved's conversion was that when he observed the liberal culture close at hand, he disliked what he saw. After graduating from Yale, Medved spent several years during the early 1970s living in Berkeley. The protest movement had already crested, but it had left behind a large residue of student radicals. "All those people who wore long hair, never bathed, spent their time protesting—I decided I didn't want to have anything to do with them," Medved said.

His views of liberals, already trending downward, reached a nadir after his apartment was robbed. The police apprehended the burglar. "It was a black kid who was twenty-four," Medved said. "It turned out that he had committed seven other burglaries."

Medved attended the trial. "I can still hear the public defender," Medved said. "She was a Jewish woman from New York. 'Travel with me now,' she said to the jury. 'Travel with me now to the impoverished backwoods of Louisiana. There is a baby crying, a black baby.' Then she went on through the whole history of slavery and oppression, as if it excused repeated acts of theft."

The jury returned a verdict of guilty, but the judge, apparently as liberal as the public defender, sentenced the burglar to just four months in jail. Medved found himself looking at the GOP's tough stance on crime with new eyes.

The third reason was Israel. When that nation suddenly found itself at war in October 1973, Medved, who had cousins in Israel, followed events closely. The first week of the war went badly. Sustaining massive losses, Israel came close to defeat. Then, warning the Soviets not to intervene, President Nixon resupplied Israel, enabling the Israelis to transform the dynamics of the war so completely that they captured the Sinai and the Golan Heights. "Democrats like McGovern, whom I had supported, said we ought to wait awhile and not rush into it," Medved said. "Not rushing into it could have cost Israel its existence." Republicans, Medved felt forced to conclude, were better friends of Israel than were Medved's fellow Democrats.

Thus the conversion of Michael Medved. He came to

believe that Jews have less to fear from evangelical Christians like those who support the GOP than from the anomie of secular culture, that liberal permissiveness is inferior to conservative firmness in confronting crime, and that Republicans are more serious than Democrats about defending Israel. Is Medved's case unique? Or are there lessons the Republican Party can learn from his experience? I fear the former.

True, there was a time in the 1970s and 1980s when it looked as though the GOP might indeed win the support of many Michael Medveds. The Democratic presidential candidates Jimmy Carter, Walter Mondale, and Michael Dukakis got Republican hopes up. Running against them, the Republican presidential candidates Gerald Ford, Ronald Reagan, and George Bush all polled more than 30 percent of the Jewish vote, considerably more than had been the Republican norm. During the same period, the neoconservatives emerged. An influential group of Republican intellectuals who used to be liberal, and in some cases radical, most of the neoconservatives were Jewish. Norman Podhoretz, editor of *Commentary,* and Irving Kristol, publisher of *The National Interest*, attracted particular attention, in part because they were important in their own right, in part because they had sons who themselves rose to prominent positions in Republican politics. John Podhoretz became a speechwriter for Ronald Reagan, William Kristol the chief of staff for Vice President Quayle. After leaving government, John Podhoretz and William Kristol founded the conservative magazine *The Weekly Standard*. Support among Jewish intellectuals, a new, higher share of the Jewish vote—at last, Republicans hoped, the GOP was gaining ground.

They were mistaken. The GOP wasn't gaining ground, the

Democratic Party was putting up bad candidates. Jimmy Carter, Walter Mondale, and Michael Dukakis appeared weak, both in their support of Israel and in their resolution to maintain our own defense, the strength of which, in turn, lends American support for Israel its credibility. Then the Democrats nominated Bill Clinton. Clinton pledged himself to the staunch support of Israel. And he promised so persuasively to uphold our own defense that he won the endorsement of no less a figure than Admiral William Crowe, the chairman of the Joint Chiefs of Staff. To the extent that Jews had ever begun a migration toward the GOP, Bill Clinton reversed it. In 1992 Bill Clinton won 78 percent of the Jewish vote, holding George Bush to just 12 percent; in 1996 Bill Clinton again won 78 percent of the Jewish vote, holding Bob Dole to just 16 percent.* As for the neoconservative movement, it remained Republican. But it also remained tiny.

Like any other institution, the Republican Party has limited resources. It therefore needs to pick and choose the groups to which it will make its strongest appeals. Since Jews cast almost the same overwhelming percentage of their votes for Bill Clinton four years ago that they cast for Franklin Roosevelt sixty-four years ago, it seems fair to conclude that they are unlikely to receive overtures from the GOP particularly warmly. What should the GOP do?

The Republican Party should oppose anti-Semitism of any kind, and it should remain explicitly committed to the well-being of Israel. But it should take those steps for the sake of its own self-respect. As for appealing to Jews, I see only two approaches. One would be to recognize that Jews have made

---

*In each election, the remainder of the Jewish vote went to third party candidates, chiefly Ross Perot.

up their minds about the GOP and to let it go at that. "The GOP has a better chance with religious Jews than secular Jews," Michael Medved said, "but do you know how few religious Jews there are? Less than 10 percent of Jews attend synagogue regularly. And even among religious Jews, most are Democrats. There's just a lot of history we're dealing with here."

Yet it is hardly in the nature of a political party to give up on an entire bloc of voters, no matter how insistently the bloc has spurned the party's advances. The Jewish population of the United States is about 5.8 million, or just a scant 600,000 more than the combined population of Iowa, Alaska, New Hampshire, and Delaware, the first states to select delegates to the national party conventions. This suggests the second approach. Like a long shot presidential candidate campaigning in those four states, the GOP would shrug off the odds, ignore the cold reception, adopt a cheerful, dogged insistence on the rightness of its cause—and go right on trying to persuade Jewish voters to support it, simply refusing to take no for an answer.

BLACK AND REPUBLICAN

The only group even more Democratic than Jews is African-Americans. This seems odd. They are the very group the Republican Party was founded to help. It was a Republican president, Abraham Lincoln, who issued the Emancipation Proclamation, freeing slaves in the Confederacy, and it was Republicans in Congress who enacted the Fourteenth Amendment, guaranteeing African-Americans the full rights of citizenship throughout the nation.

It isn't as if African-Americans were ungrateful. For decades after the Civil War, they proved overwhelmingly Republican. In the South, where most black people remained after the war, literacy tests, poll taxes, and other Jim Crow laws limited the ability of black people to express their allegiance to either party. Yet when they did vote, they voted for the GOP. According to Seymour Martin Lipset, as late as 1932 black people gave a majority of their votes to the Republican presidential candidate, Herbert Hoover, even as Hoover was losing to the Democratic candidate, Franklin Roosevelt, in a landslide.

African-Americans first became Democratic for the same reason as did Jews: the Great Depression. The poorest people in the nation, black people needed help even more badly than did anyone else, and the New Deal gave it to them. By 1936, black people had changed their allegiance from the Republican to the Democratic Party, giving Franklin Roosevelt nearly 90 percent of their vote. They have been giving Democrats huge margins ever since.

Yet this still seems odd. Why should African-Americans have provided such consistent support to the Democratic Party over so many decades? Black people are in many ways conservative. They go to church. They favor tough measures against crime. Jews may fear that Republicans are anti-Semites, but do black people have any reason to suppose there are more racists in the Republican Party than in the Democratic Party? When it was the Democratic Party that promulgated Jim Crow? I have come across only one explanation for the loyalty of African-Americans to the Democratic Party that makes any sense. African-Americans want big government.

There are three reasons why they should. The first is obvious. After centuries of slavery and then decades of Jim Crow, black people want the government to be big in order to protect their civil rights. The second reason is that black people are the poorest ethnic group in the nation. Black households are the most likely, in particular, to be headed by single parents, most often mothers—in 1998, 64 percent of African-American children under the age of eighteen were in households headed by single mothers. Black people therefore feel a need for welfare, food stamps, and the whole panoply of public assistance that big government provides. The third reason is that so many African-Americans hold government jobs. While just one in five white Americans with college degrees works for the government, three in five African-Americans with college degrees do so. African-Americans thus feel the same affinity for big government that autoworkers feel for GM and Ford or steelworkers feel for U.S. Steel. Big government sends home the paycheck.

While the Democratic Party has been busy providing the big government that African-Americans seek, the GOP has scarcely even gone to the effort of making itself look welcoming. In 1896, the black Republican George H. White was elected to the House of Representatives from North Carolina. After White left office in 1901, it was 27 years before the election to the House of the next black Republican, Oscar De Priest of Illinois. After De Priest left Congress in 1935, it was another thirty-two years before the arrival of the next black Republican, Senator Edward Brooke of Massachusetts. When Brooke retired in 1979, it was 12 years before the black Republican Gary Franks of Connecticut arrived in the House, to be joined there in 1995 by the black Republican J. C. Watts of Oklahoma, who, since Franks left office in 1996, is the only black Republican member of Congress. One century. A grand total of five black Republicans in Congress. The Democrats had dozens. If you're an African-American, you don't need a doctorate in political science to know which party is yours.

As it happens, Justin Adams, a thirty-year-old African-American, is actually studying for a doctorate, although his degree will be granted in political economics, not political science. He is fit, handsome, well-spoken, and obviously intelligent—altogether so impressive that one of the first questions I asked when I got to know him was why he had decided to spend precious years pursuing a Ph.D. at Stanford when he could have his pick of lucrative jobs in Silicon Valley. We will come to Justin's reply in a moment.

Justin's mother grew up in the North, his father in the South. Both struggled to get an education. His mother worked in a library, where she read widely, trying to improve her mind. She succeeded, winning the single scholarship that her high school offered to Wayne State University. His father put himself through the University of Minnesota. "The things he went through," Justin said one evening over dinner. "What things?" I asked. Justin grimaced, preferring not to go into it. "Let's just say this," Justin answered. "He essentially worked his ass off and mastered the material, and the professors gave him Cs, because that was the grade to give a black student. It was an impetus. It just made him work harder."

Justin's father works in the aerospace industry in Southern California. During the most important years of Justin's childhood, Justin's family lived in Orange County. Now, Orange County is affluent, educated, and new—just forty years ago the county, which has a population of more than 2.5 million, amounted to little more than orange groves and cattle ranches. Orange County is thus about as far as you can get from the prejudices of insular southern towns or the segregated neighborhoods of northern cities—or so I imagined. Justin corrected me. There was so much racism in his Orange County neighborhood, he explained, that his parents never let him or his siblings play in their front yard for fear of exposing them to taunts. Once, playing a prank with some white kids in the neighborhood, Justin's older brother helped to remove the hubcaps from a car. The owner of the car ignored the white kids, marched to Justin's house and stood in the driveway, shouting racial slurs.

Justin was raised a Democrat. "We were black, so we were Democrats," Justin says. "That's the way it worked." When he got to be old enough to think about politics for himself, being a Democrat still made sense. "When I was becoming politically aware," Justin says, "Reagan was in office. I don't know. You just didn't get the sense from Republicans that they cared about minorities."

After getting a Stanford master's degree in political science, Justin decided his knowledge of politics was too abstract. He wanted to see politics in action. So in 1994 he moved to Sacramento, where he held a series of jobs in the state government. First he served as an intern in the governor's Office of Planning and Research. Even as Justin went to work for the Republican governor, Pete Wilson, he supported Wilson's opponent in the November election, the Democratic candidate for governor, Kathleen Brown. Then Justin began getting to know the state government a little better. The first shock hit him when he spent a year at the Department of Housing and Community Development. "They made loans to low-income families," Justin explained. "But they were essentially grants rather than loans, because no one ever spent any time trying to get these people to pay them back. It was outrageous."

Next Justin spent a year at Caltrans, the state transportation department. There he discovered another rich picture of Your Tax Dollars At Work. Caltrans had seventeen thousand employees and an annual budget of $6 billion. "It was the bureaucracy of bureaucracies," Justin said. The department's employees divided neatly into two categories. The first was comprised of employees who were inert. "There were a whole lot of people you just had to say were deadwood. They spent a lot of time just playing computer games at their desks." The second category was comprised of engineers. They spent their days designing highways, bridges, and railroad lines that they intended to build for the people of California at a cost of tens of billions of dollars whether the people of California needed them or not. "It was primarily an engineering culture," Justin said. "They didn't want to hear about costs."

What he saw of big government made Justin feel uneasy with the party of big government. Two ballot initiatives forced him to act upon his unease, voting with the GOP, then joining it.

The first was Proposition 187, on the ballot in 1994. Proposition 187, as we have seen, would have denied all but emergency services to illegal immigrants. To his own astonishment, Justin found himself supporting it. "I had a friend [in the governor's office] who was crunching the numbers," Justin explained. The cost to California of providing illegal immigrants with schooling, health care, and other services each year, Justin's friend informed him, was between $3 and $4 billion—almost 10 percent of the general fund. Since his own family had been subjected to prejudice, Justin knew what immigrants were going through. He sympathized with them. He always had. But now that he knew the costs that illegal immigrants were imposing on law-abiding citizens, Justin found himself thinking thoughts that had never before entered his mind. He understood how hard his parents had worked to buy their home and provide for their children. That the state government was taking their money to provide for people who had entered the country in flagrant violation of the law—the very idea was infuriating. "Governor Wilson went out of his way to make it clear that the issue wasn't immigration per se," Justin says. "The issue was *illegal* immigration. How can it be right for people who are here illegally to cost everybody else billions every year?"

In 1994, Justin voted for both Proposition 187 and for the Republican Pete Wilson, who had endorsed it.

Two years later, in 1996, Proposition 209 appeared on the ballot. Proposition 209 called for an end to all affirmative action throughout the state government. Before election day, when the proposition would be voted on, Governor Wilson took matters a step further. Lobbying the regents of the University of California, Wilson proposed abolishing affirmative action throughout the entire UC system. Wilson's proposal proved inflammatory. Proponents argued that admission into the UC system should be based on academic qualifications alone. Opponents claimed that if Wilson's proposal was adopted, black and Hispanic enrollment in the UC system would plummet. Justin found himself torn. "Initially I was opposed to ending affirmative action," he says. But as he thought about it, what kept coming to mind was how hard his parents had worked, making their way into the middle class on their own merits. "Finally I decided that I supported the measure," Justin said. "Nobody should be *guaranteed* a spot in a university."

The regents adopted Governor Wilson's proposal, abolishing affirmative action throughout the UC system.* Then the California electorate, including Justin Adams, approved Proposition 209. Both measures were challenged in court. If Justin had had any lingering doubts about opposing affirmative action, the legal challenges, which ultimately failed, dispelled them. "The argument was that the measures discriminated against minorities because they didn't allow race to be taken into account," Justin said. "Being color-blind was somehow supposed to be discriminatory. It seemed completely idiotic to me."

Propositions 187 and 209 proved polarizing. "You were either for them or against them. I finally decided I was for them," Justin says. Not long after voting for Proposition 209, Justin registered as a Republican.

Justin Adams is of course exceptional—few members of any ethnic group make it into doctoral programs at universities as prominent as Stanford. Yet there are other Justin Adamses. Lots of them. African-Americans are moving into the middle class. Consider a couple of statistics. Forty-two percent of all black people and 75 percent of married black

---

*Since racial preferences were abolished in the UC system, black and Hispanic enrollment has indeed dropped at certain schools, including the two most selective institutions in the system, Berkeley and UCLA, but it has increased at other schools, including UC San Diego. As the black conservative Thomas Sowell writes, "it was virtually inevitable that minority students would redistribute themselves among institutions. But the black and Hispanic students who no longer went to Berkeley did not disappear into thin air or fail to go to college at all. UC San Diego is not chopped liver."

couples own their own homes. Nearly a third live in the sub-urbs. In 1998 the number of black people who said they were better off at the end of the year than they had been at the beginning exceeded the number of whites who said so, indi-cating that African-Americans are benefiting from the current expansion—and know it.

Here I have to take back part of what I said earlier. African-Americans do indeed want big government—African-Americans who still have not made their way into the middle class. But African-Americans who are already in the middle class look on big government with different eyes. They have experienced that most American of phenomena—hard work paying off. They feel a certain security in their position and abilities. Although they of course want the government to protect their civil rights, they know that racism has lost its power to hold African-Americans down. They don't need pub-lic assistance for the obvious reason that they're doing just fine. Many still work for the government, but a large and growing proportion work in the private sector.

The Republican Party will probably never hold much ap-peal for African-Americans outside the middle class. Reform welfare? Abolish affirmative action? No politician I can think of would volunteer to run on that platform in Harlem or Watts. Yet even without trying—and Lord knows it hasn't tried—the GOP appears to have won a surprising amount of sup-port in the African-American middle class already. "Ordinarily a Republican is doing really well if he gets 10 percent of the black vote," Jim McLaughlin, president of the polling com-pany Fabrizio, McLaughlin and Associates told me. "But when you poll middle-class blacks, a lot of the time you'll see a real jump in the numbers." No one has performed a re-liable nationwide survey of middle-class African-Americans,

McLaughlin explained, so the evidence is only anecdotal. But the evidence all points one way: Middle-class African-Americans are more Republican than African-Americans as a whole. Recalling work his firm did for George Allen, the former Republican governor of Virginia, and James Gilmore, the current Republican governor of Virginia, McLaughlin said, "When we polled middle-class blacks, almost 20 percent supported Allen and Gilmore. In some places middle-class blacks voted Republican at almost the same rate as middle-class whites."

If for a change the Republican Party were actually to make a concerted effort to appeal to African-Americans, what should it do? Justin Adams provides a clue.

If his parents imparted one value to their children, Justin told me, it was the importance of education. Justin's parents went over their homework with Justin, his brother, and his two sisters every night. During the summers, when the neighborhood white children were playing games in the street or spending days at Disneyland, Justin's parents made their own children continue their studies. "My parents bought a big chalkboard to drill the four of us children over the summer," Justin says. "It's still in the house." His parents so impressed on him the importance of education that Justin feels compelled to get just as much education as his abilities permit. This is why he's working on his doctorate. The fat jobs in high tech will have to wait.

Although Justin's family took matters further than most—Justin's older brother got an MS in electrical engineering while his younger sister received a doctorate in molecular biology—polls indicate that black people across the country place the same importance on education. Yet a disproportionate number of black children are consigned to the country's worst public schools. Force people who value education to send their children to bad public schools, and what do you get? Support for vouchers. Almost half of African-Americans support vouchers—one of the highest proportions of any ethnic group.

How do vouchers work? Each year parents receive a check—that is, a voucher—for roughly the same amount that it costs to educate each of their school-age children in a public school. The parents may spend that money enrolling their children at the school of their choice—a public school, a charter school, a religious school, a technical school, or any other school. Vouchers face bitter opposition from teachers' unions, which in turn represent an important constituency of the Democratic Party. Indeed, teachers' unions have fought voucher initiatives so fiercely—when a voucher initiative appeared on the California ballot in 1993, the California Teachers Association spent some $10 million campaigning against it—that voucher programs have been put into effect in only a handful of communities.

In 1992, during his first campaign for mayor of Jersey City, New Jersey, the Republican Bret Schundler went door-to-door in his city, explaining vouchers to parents, many of whom were African-American. He told them that a public school education for each of their children cost $9,000 a year. Then he asked if they believed they could get a better education for their children if they were simply given the money and permitted to spend it on any school they chose. "Not one parent said, 'I don't understand,'" Schundler has written. "Instead they replied, 'Thank God.'"

Supporting vouchers would permit the GOP to prosper, gaining support among middle-class African-Americans while helping children who would otherwise attend bad public schools. Yet Republican politicians have tended to shut their eyes, imagine the ferocious, well-funded opposition from teachers' unions that voucher plans would engender, then surprise themselves with the number of other proposals they can come up with instead. Bret Schundler has found it impossible to get a voucher plan through the New Jersey legislature—a body controlled by Republicans. The only voucher plan a Republican has managed to enact was signed into law last year by Governor Jeb Bush of Florida. According to Bush's legislation, vouchers will be given to parents whose children attend the state's worst public schools—but only after the schools have failed to meet certain standards in two out of four years.

The GOP might never give vouchers the support they deserve. Never underestimate the ability of Republicans to miss an opportunity. On the other hand, who knows? In their heart of hearts, in my experience, a surprising number of Republicans would actually like to do some good.

THE CATHOLICS

David Brady was raised in Kankakee, Illinois, one of six children in a Catholic family of Irish, German, and French descent. His father worked at the General Mills factory. His mother sent all the children to parochial schools, and every Sunday she scrubbed them, dressed them in their best clothes, and walked them—the family couldn't afford a car—to church. Both David's parents were Democrats. I asked David over lunch if his family took its membership in the Democratic Party seriously. David replied with a story.

"My mother was one of fourteen children," David said,

"so the kids in our family had a lot of aunts and uncles. But the one we loved best was our uncle Ray. He'd fought in the Second World War, and he'd come home with a lot of loot—a couple of Japanese guns, some Japanese helmets, stuff like that. He'd show that stuff to us kids, and we loved it. Then Uncle Ray did something bad. He voted for Eisenhower. He said he liked Ike as a general. I can remember lying in bed and overhearing the grown-ups arguing about it. For a long time, nobody talked to Uncle Ray—even a kid like me wasn't allowed to talk to him. It was like he'd been excommunicated. Hell, yes, we took the Democratic Party seriously."

We are dealing here with white Catholics—that is, Catholics who are neither African-American nor Hispanic. (African-Americans and Hispanics are so distinctive that they have to be dealt with separately, African-Americans above, Hispanics in a later chapter.) The Irish and Germans got here first, beginning to arrive in large numbers in the 1840s. The Irish came to escape the potato famine. The Germans came for a variety of reasons, but their desire to escape being pressed into military service by one or another of the petty German principalities should not be underestimated. Virtually all the Irish were Catholics. Most of them remained in cities as laborers. (Some of the few who became farmers, as it happens, settled near my grandfather, who was a farmer himself. He also operated a water-powered sawmill that, each fall, with the rearranging of some belts and pulleys, became an apple press. Good teetotaling Baptist that he was, my grandfather pretended he didn't know that when the Irish brought him their apples to press, they intended to use the juice to make hard cider. "What did he say they were going to use it for?" I once asked my mother. She replied, "Gallons and gallons of vinegar.") Like all urban laborers, the Irish became Democrats. If anything set them apart, it was the aplomb with which they did so, simply transferring the animosity they felt toward the English lords who had oppressed them for centuries in the Old World to the WASP Whigs, and, after the formation of the GOP, WASP Republicans whom they found looking down on them in the New. (David Brady, who thinks of himself as mostly Irish, retains this animosity toward WASPs in a remarkably pure form. If you want to get off to a bad start at a meeting with David, show up dressed like a preppie. You'll have to endure his gibes about penny loafers and Brooks Brothers clothes before you can get down to business.)

The German story is more complicated. Immigrants from northern Germany were Protestants. Identifying with the Protestants they found here, they tended to become Whigs, and, later, Republicans. Immigrants from southern Germany were Catholics. Yet many moved to the countryside to become farmers and often, once again, Whigs, then Republicans. German Catholics who remained in the cities became, like the Irish, Democrats. Then they underwent a final subdivision at the time of the First World War. Although they had been unhappy enough with Germany to leave, they were nevertheless aghast when the United States waged war on their homeland. Seeing the conflict as a Democratic war—Woodrow Wilson, a Democrat, was president—many German Catholics became Republicans. The remnant that in spite of the war against their homeland remained Democratic, it seems safe to assume, remained very Democratic.

Nearly all the rest of the white Catholics arrived, along with additional Irish and German immigrants, during the great wave of immigration between roughly 1880 and 1924—indeed, aside from the Jews, most of those who came during the great wave were Catholics. Still poor newcomers during the 1930s, the Italians, Poles, Hungarians, Czechs, and the most recent Irish and German arrivals found themselves won over by Franklin Roosevelt and the New Deal and, like Jews and African-Americans, gave their allegiance to the Democratic Party, the party of the little man.

From the New Deal to the 1960s, white Catholics voted solidly Democratic with just one exception, the 1956 presidential matchup between Eisenhower and Adlai Stevenson, when Catholics gave Ike 51 percent of their vote—David Brady's uncle Ray wasn't the only Catholic miscreant that year. Catholic loyalty to the Democratic Party peaked four years later, when the Irish Catholic, John Kennedy, ran for president against the Anglo-Saxon Quaker, Richard Nixon. Kennedy took 78 percent of the Catholic vote. "I licked envelopes for Jack Kennedy," David Brady says. "He was good-looking, he was articulate, he got into Harvard, and he was one of us. What more could you ask?"

Since the election of 1960, the loyalty of white Catholics to the Democratic Party has tailed off. There are a couple of reasons for this. One is that Catholics have changed. They used to receive less education than Protestants, perform blue-collar work, and live in ethnic enclaves. Now Catholics are just as educated as Protestants, perform nearly as much white-collar work, and are almost as likely to live in the suburbs. As Catholics have come to look more like Protestants, they have come to vote more like Protestants, too. The second reason is that the Democratic Party has changed. It would have been unthinkable in 1960 for John Kennedy to have supported gay rights or abortion. It would be just as unthinkable in 2000 for Ted Kennedy not to do so. For many Catholics, the Democratic Party has simply become too liberal.

After graduating from high school, David Brady remained in his hometown of Kankakee to take a job in a furniture factory. Then he mauled his hand in a belt on the assembly line. He had to spend months recuperating. The gruesome accident changed his life—amazingly enough, for the better. Since he had time to spare and a little money in his pocket—the union made sure he received disability pay—David spent a few days visiting a high school friend who was studying at Western Illinois Teachers' College. "All he did was read books and go to parties," David says. "I thought, 'This beats working in a factory.'" David dropped by the admissions office to find out what he had to do to get in. All he needed was a diploma from an Illinois high school, "a requirement I had barely managed to meet." The next fall David enrolled, beginning an academic career that would make him one of the leading political scientists in the country and a full professor at Stanford University. Like millions of other Catholics, David escaped the blue-collar enclave in which he was raised and ended up living like a Protestant.

If David illustrates the first reason Catholic loyalty to the Democratic Party eroded, that Catholics themselves changed, he also illustrates the second, that the Democratic Party moved too far to the left. David being David, he reached this conclusion circuitously. Studying for his doctorate at the University of Iowa, he became a Marxist.

"You?" I asked.

"Don't look so surprised. Marxism was a serious intellectual endeavor, and at one point in my life I was a serious intellectual."

Attempting to put his Marxism into practice, David joined the anti-war movement. During one protest, he was arrested, although, since he was paying for school by working on construction sites and had therefore never grown long hair or a beard, he had to beg the cops, some of whom were Irish, and who recognized a decent Catholic boy when they saw one, to drag him off to jail along with the more bedraggled protesters. At first the protests in which David participated were peaceful. Then they grew violent. When they did, David dropped out of the anti-war movement. "The kids were coordinating their movements with walkie-talkies, smashing windows, serious stuff. During one of the protests some fat cop had a heart attack. I figured the Vietnam War wasn't *his* fault," David said.

Growing uneasy with what he saw of Marxism in practice, David began to wonder about Marxism in theory. "The idea was that workers would all be brothers if only they were freed from class oppressors. It didn't seem to be working out that way in the Soviet Union. Ho Chi Minh wasn't such a nice guy. Mao killed maybe 40 million people, maybe more. Stuff like that starts to add up. You say to yourself, 'Wait a minute. Let's think this over again.'"

David read extensively in economics, finding himself impressed by the work of Milton Friedman. Then, pursuing his specialty, the politics of government regulation, David realized that the more he learned, the more he concluded that government regulations, no matter how well-meaning, distort markets so badly that they almost always do more harm than good. By the time he moved to Texas to teach at the University of Houston, he was a conservative. "That's what happened. I became a conservative first. Turning into a Republican came second."

It also came hard. On election day 1980, David stepped inside the voting booth intending to cast his ballot for Ronald Reagan. It would be the first time in his life he had voted for a Republican. He put his hand up to the lever. He couldn't pull it.

"I saw my father's face," David explained. "He was saying, 'Son, what are you doing? You know you can't vote for a *Republican.*'" A widely regarded political scientist, David walked out without casting a vote.

Four years later, in 1984, David once again stepped inside the voting booth intending to cast his ballot for Ronald Reagan. But his father appeared to him again. This time when David left without voting, he got a pass that would permit him to return later in the day. He figured all he needed was a couple of hours to get his nerve up. "I called a buddy in Washington who was a pollster. He told me it was shaping up as a landslide for Reagan. Once I knew that—once I was *sure* Mondale was going to lose—I went back and voted for Mondale."

In 1986 David received an appointment at Stanford. "One of the first things I do when I move to a new place is try to figure out the local politics," David said. He attended a Democratic meeting to hear Barbara Boxer, then a member of Congress from Marin County, north of San Francisco, and now one of California's two senators. "I sat in the front row. The stuff she said was so wacko, so far to the left, I had to bury my face in my hands. I was embarrassed for her." David felt certain everyone in the audience felt just as he did, but since he was in the front row he couldn't tell. "You have to remember, I'd just spent years in Texas. Democrats there aren't like Democrats in the rest of the country. They would never have put up with that kind of left-wing stuff." Yet instead of hearing the audience behind him razz Boxer when she finished, David heard the sounds of a standing ovation. "I couldn't believe it. I hung around for half an hour afterward talking to people to find out what they believed. Sure enough, they were all just as far to the left as Boxer."

The next day, David registered as a Republican. One more white Catholic had decided that the Democratic Party was too liberal.

The GOP once thought Catholics like David Brady would come to it en masse. In 1980 Ronald Reagan became the first Republican presidential candidate since Ike to win a majority of the Catholic vote, polling 51 percent. Four years later Reagan polled 57 percent of the Catholic vote. By the time George Bush won 56 percent of the Catholic vote in 1988, the GOP believed that Reagan Democrats—the millions of Democrats who crossed party lines to vote for Reagan in 1980 and 1984, many of whom were white Catholics—were becoming Bush Republicans. Instead, the Reagan Democrats became Clinton Democrats. Running against Clinton in 1992, Bush saw his share of the Catholic vote plummet to 37 percent. Four years later, Dole polled only 40 percent. Yet by contrast with Jews, who, since Clinton has headed the Democratic Party, have once again become faithful Democrats, Catholics have returned to the Democratic Party only provisionally. In 1994 Catholics gave a majority of their vote, 53 percent, to Republican congressional candidates, enabling the GOP to recapture the House of Representatives for the first time in forty years. Just two years after helping Clinton win the White House, in other words, Catholics helped Republicans humiliate him.

Catholics have thus become swing voters. They take stands

on the issues that cut across both parties. Catholics—especially, polls show, those who attend church regularly—oppose abortion. That inclines them toward the GOP. Yet they support health care and welfare while opposing the death penalty. That inclines them toward the Democratic Party. (Plenty of Democrats, including President Clinton, support the death penalty, but eliminating the death penalty still has more support among Democrats than among Republicans.) Catholics might as well be playing peekaboo with Republicans and Democrats alike. Now you see us, now you don't.

How can the GOP appeal to Catholics?

"Study Reagan," David Brady replied.

Catholics voted for Reagan for many reasons that were peculiar to Reagan himself. Reagan was Irish. He grew up in the Midwest, where many Catholics live, and he kept the simple manners of the Midwest all his life. "He may not have been Catholic," David Brady said, "but he seemed like us. He was a guy you knew you'd like to go out with for a couple of beers." But those weren't the only reasons Catholics supported him.

"Reagan had a good heart," David continued. "That was a lot more important than you might think." Although Catholics have moved up in the world, they still feel a particular sympathy for the little man. They're just a couple of generations away from the immigrant experience. And their church teaches a "preferential option for the poor," arguing that society should be judged at least in part on the way it treats its most unfortunate members. It made a difference to Catholics that Reagan was able to cut taxes and retard the growth of government spending without conveying ill will toward the poor and disadvantaged.

"People could claim that Reagan was mean-spirited, but

it just wouldn't stick," David said. "I mean, you could see just to look at him that he wasn't. Now compare Reagan with some of the Republicans who came after him. Newt Gingrich? Give me a break."

Now that Reagan was gone, David said, the GOP needed to get rid of the spokesmen who were giving it an ugly face. Dumping Gingrich was a good start. (Strictly speaking, Gingrich wasn't dumped from the speakership of the House of Representatives, he resigned. But Republican members of the House were so dissatisfied with him that they probably *would* have dumped him.) "Then I think that the GOP has to keep talking," David continued. "Republicans have to say, 'Maybe welfare isn't such a great idea, but because it hurts the people who are on it, not because the Republican Party is a bunch of sixty-year-old WASPs who have got it made and stopped caring about anybody else. Maybe it's better for people's self-respect if they develop skills, get a job, and learn how to show up for work every day instead of taking government handouts.'

"The GOP's ideas are right," David continued. "The free market *is* better than big government. But the GOP has to say it believes in the free market for the right reasons—because the market is better for everybody, even the poor, not just for fat cats.

"Can Republicans learn to talk like that?" David asked. "Beats me. But if they want the Catholic vote, they'd better."

Journal entry:
I still can't imagine doing what each of them has done. Michael Medved and David Brady have friends who suggest

only half-jokingly that they must have been out of their minds to become Republicans. For Justin Adams, it has been even worse.

"To most black people," Justin says, "I'm a sellout. It's not as if every time I meet a black person I say, 'Hey, did I happen to tell you what political party I belong to?' But people find out. And I know what they think of me when they do."

It's astonishing. It really is. There are people to whom being a Republican is so important that they're willing to pay a price.

Chapter Six

A TALE OF TWO CITIES

Journal entry:

As the plane banked to land in Washington, D.C., this afternoon, I found myself peering out the window to admire the Capitol far below. The building has always struck me as a kind of architectural miracle. Virtually none of Benjamin Latrobe's original structure remains visible—the north and south wings, in which the Senate and House now sit, were added in the mid-nineteenth century, while much of the construction of the dome took place later, during the Civil War—yet somehow each successive architect got everything right, making certain that his own changes enhanced rather than distorted the design. If only, I found myself wishing, the country had been as fortunate in the changes that have been made to Congress itself.

The Constitution originally mandated one member of the House of Representatives for every thirty thousand inhabitants of the country. For several decades that formula gave the House a relatively small membership—the first time the body met it was comprised of just fifty-nine representatives. But as the country grew, so did the House. By the second half of the nineteenth century, when the membership of the House had grown to more than three hundred, observers began to argue that the institution was becoming unwieldy. By the early years of the twentieth cen-

tury, when the membership of the House had grown to more than four hundred, even congressmen themselves could see that the institution would soon be teetering on the brink of chaos. Congress acted in 1929. Yet instead of shrinking the House to make the institution collegial once again, Congress simply froze the membership at 435. And there the House has remained, teetering on the brink of chaos ever since.

As the plane floated toward the runway, it struck me that the size of the House in itself puts the Republicans who serve there at a disadvantage. Republicans like order. Chaos is for Democrats.

The two cities to which the title of this chapter refers are Washington, D.C., and Jersey City, New Jersey, both of which I visited to investigate a question that had been puzzling me for months. Why do Republicans in the House of Representatives so often look hangdog or bewildered, while Republican governors and mayors—including the Republican mayor of Jersey City—so often appear to be enjoying themselves?

In Washington, I talked with three prominent Republicans, one a former member of the House, ex-Speaker Newt Gingrich, and two who are current members of the House, Congressman Henry Hyde of Illinois and Congressman Christopher Cox of California.

OPERATOR? GET ME ST. HELENA

If you do not remember the excitement that Republicans felt back in 1994 when the GOP captured the House of Representatives for the first time in forty years, take my word for it. We whooped and hollered. At the election night party that I attended, Republicans embraced, tears in their eyes, then drank round after round to celebrate, then embraced again, even tearier. President Clinton had been repudiated. The Democrats were down and we were up. Since the powers of the Senate majority leader are for the most part administrative, the most powerful Republican in America—the leader of us all—was the man who would soon be sworn in as speaker of the house, Congressman Newt Gingrich of Georgia. All hail, Newt!

Six years later the Republican majority in the House has shrunk from twenty-six seats to just 11, giving the GOP the slimmest majority held by either party in the House in forty-seven years. Republicans in the House now lack even the semblance of a coherent agenda, much less a ten-point program such as the Contract with America on which they swept to victory in 1994. And Newt Gingrich himself is out of a job, having resigned from the House after the GOP's feeble showing in the 1998 election, during which, polls showed, voters regarded him as one of the most unpopular politicians in the nation.

What went wrong? When I posed the question to Gingrich himself, he answered, in effect, nothing.

"Go back and look at the assumptions of Washington in the summer of 1994," Gingrich said. Everyone in Washington—the administration, Congress, the press—believed the federal government would run $200 billion a year deficits indefinitely, that taxes would continue to go up, that welfare would remain an unreformed mess, and that federal spending would continue to grow. "Now look at the accomplishments of the last five years," Gingrich said. The federal budget is in surplus, taxes have been trimmed, welfare has been reformed, and although federal spending has indeed continued to grow, the economy has grown even faster, so that relative to the private sector the government outlays have actually shrunk.

"It's like a movement in plate tectonics," Gingrich said. His hair looked grayer than I remembered it from television, but other than that Newt was Newt—intense, voluble, self-assured. "We shifted the basic nature of American government about ten points to the right."

If Republicans had scored such a success, then why had the GOP seen its majority in the House reduced in the election of 1996, then reduced again in 1998? Why had Gingrich found himself forced to step down as speaker?

"I was representing a proactive agenda executed through the legislative branch in opposition to the executive branch," Gingrich replied. In other words, Gingrich was behaving as though he, and not Bill Clinton, was the president. "We pulled that off for three years, from 1994 through some of 1997. That's probably as long as anybody in American history has ever been able to do it."

While Speaker Gingrich was spending those three years attempting to force President Clinton to cut programs and balance the budget, House Republicans saw their popularity plummet. The low moment took place during the government shutdown of 1995. Intent on balancing the budget, Gingrich gave Clinton a choice: either accept a Republican budget or close the government. Clinton closed the government. Functions considered "essential" continued—the Pentagon stayed open, Social Security checks continued to be put in the mail, and so on. But a great many "inessential" functions did indeed cease. The Smithsonian shut down. The National Parks closed. Gingrich was certain the public would blame the president. The public blamed the House Republicans instead. Although they had been hoping to increase their majority in the elections of 1996, the House Republicans lost eight seats instead. Their morale has never recovered. But what Gingrich sees when he looks at this record is success. "Now, for one wave of change," he said, "what we accomplished is a hell of a deal."

Almost the moment my interview with him came to an end, it struck me that Gingrich was America's answer to Napoleon Bonaparte.

I do not mean to poke fun at Gingrich when I say this. I mean that the parallels between the two men are truly striking. Napoleon rose to power during a period of uncertainty and indecision in France, unifying the nation by demonstrating tactical brilliance and an indomitable will. As emperor, he remade the politics of Europe. But Napoleon overreached, embarking upon a project—crossing the entire continent of Europe to conquer the vast landmass of Russia—that one look at the map demonstrates to have been mad. Likewise Gingrich. He rose to power in the GOP when the party was still reeling from the defeat of George Bush, demonstrating Napoleon-like tactical brilliance and an indomitable will as he unified Republicans, then led them to victory. As speaker, he remade American politics, not as dramatically, to be sure, as Napoleon remade the politics of France, but nevertheless shifting American politics considerably to the right, just as he claimed when he spoke to me. But Gingrich overreached, embarking upon a project—turning the speakership into a "counterpresidency," as George Will puts it—that a glance at American history shows the founders never intended and no speaker has ever been able to sustain.

According to the notes of the small court of flatterers that accompanied him into exile, to listen to Napoleon hold forth on St. Helena you would have thought he was still emperor and that the catastrophic winter retreat from Moscow had never taken place. Once again, likewise Gingrich. He continues to radiate certitude so convincingly that when you listen to him you find yourself believing that only the victories mattered and that the defeats—the loss of morale, the shrunken majority, the way the public came to see Republicans in the House not as idealistic reformers but as hardhearted zealots—were all irrelevant.

Which brings us back to the Republicans in the House. To understand their present state of mind, it helps to think of them as veterans of the Grande Armée. After all that Gingrich put them through, they might as well have trod barefoot through the snows of Russia.

IMPEACHMENT, ANYONE?

Journal entry:
Searching for the office of Congressman Henry Hyde today, I got lost, coming to a stop at a T in one of the Rayburn Building's dozens of identical marble hallways. For a moment I was completely disoriented. Then I smelled it. Cigar smoke. I followed the scent straight to Hyde's office.

In my experience there are two kinds of people who smoke cigars. The first kind is the arrogant jerk, a category that would include many Wall Street tycoons and southern sheriffs. Jerks like to lord it over others, and for them cigar smoke is an assertion of power. The second kind is the old gaffer, a category that would include one of my favorite great-uncles. They don't mean anyone any harm. They picked up the cigar habit when they were young and still think of cigars as an innocent pleasure. Henry Hyde? After the impeachment proceedings, millions of Americans, who saw in Hyde a man maniacally bent on getting President Clinton, would assume that Hyde is the first kind of cigar smoker, the arrogant jerk. (One of the reasons I wrote this book is that during the impeachment proceedings my agent asked how a nice guy like me could belong to the same party as a jerk—he actually used the word—like Henry Hyde.) But after spending an hour with Hyde, I can tell you that he's actually the second kind of cigar smoker, the old gaffer. I'll go further than that. He's one of the most appealing old gaffers I've ever met.

When I walked into his office, Hyde was seated at his desk. The desk was heaped so high with letters, legal pads, mementos, newspapers, and other items that it looked as if the janitor had emptied a wastebasket on top of it the night before. Placed atop the desktop clutter—it would have been impossible to clear a space for it—lay a large, amber ashtray in which sat a lit cigar. Hyde stood to greet me happily. More than six feet tall and approaching, by my estimate, 260 pounds, Hyde wore a rumpled dark suit with suspenders in place of a belt. When I asked for permission to record our conversation, Hyde replied, "Tape away, tape away!" with an air of amused theatricality. The mane of white hair, the jollity— Hyde reminded me of Frank Morgan playing the Wizard of Oz, not the great and terrible Oz who frightened Dorothy and her friends, but the lovable old man behind the curtain.

As chairman of the House Judiciary Committee, Hyde

conducted the hearings into the impeachment of President Clinton, then served as leader of the House managers during the Senate trial of the president. Puffing his cigar, Hyde answered every question about the impeachment proceedings that I put to him.

Had the proceedings hurt him in his district? Hyde couldn't say. "I never took a poll. I had a duty to perform as chairman of the Judiciary Committee regardless of the wishes of my district."

Had Hyde known just how bad the House managers looked on television? All eleven were white Christian males. Opposite them on the floor of the Senate, President Clinton's defense team included an African-American woman, a Jew, and, in Charles Ruff, the eloquent White House counsel, a man in a wheelchair. The contest looked like eleven curmudgeons in bad suits taking on . . . the people. Hyde had indeed known just how bad it looked. But there had been nothing he could do about it. All the managers, he explained, were drawn from the Republicans on the House Judiciary Committee, a group that, with just one exception, was made up entirely of white Christian males. The exception was Mary Bono, who was completing the term of her husband, Sonny Bono, after his death in a skiing accident the previous winter. Not even a lawyer, Bono had only served on the committee a matter of months. "If I had put her on it would have been an affirmative action move," Hyde said. "I didn't want to be hypocritical. So we did the best we could with what we had."

Hyde proved thoughtful, equable. I couldn't even get him to criticize the independent counsel, Kenneth Starr. Believe me, I tried.

Starr spent many years and tens of millions of dollars conducting investigations, I said. He probed Whitewater, in which the Clintons are alleged to have participated in defrauding a savings and loan institution; Travelgate, in which, as part of a plan to give contracts for government travel to Clinton cronies, the administration used the FBI to sully the reputations of the innocent civil servants who were running the White House travel office; and Filegate, in which Clinton operatives directed the FBI to give the White House nine hundred files on members of the Reagan and Bush administrations. Whitewater, Travelgate, Filegate. All three involved allegations of serious wrongdoing, and two of the three, Travelgate and Filegate, involved gross abuses of presidential power. Yet when Kenneth Starr finally delivered his referral to Congress, it contained nothing but thousands of pages of Monica. Monica snapping her thong at the president. Monica talking dirty to the president. Monica performing sexual acts on the president while he spoke on the telephone to members of Congress. Henry Hyde served a long and honorable career in the House. Then Kenneth Starr decided to cap Hyde's career with smut.

"Weren't you disappointed when you learned that Starr's referral dealt with nothing but Monica?" I asked.

"Yes," Hyde replied. "We all wondered what had happened to the other scandals, especially Travelgate and Filegate, since there were so many patently bizarre aspects to both of those."

"Then don't you believe that Starr should have done a better job? Don't you believe that his referral should have included the other scandals?"

Hyde puffed his cigar. He replied pleasantly. "I've not talked about it with Mr. Starr. I look forward to having that conversation with him someday."

Only once was I able to get Henry Hyde to mete out any

blame. He fixed it on himself. When the Senate refused to permit the House managers to stage a genuine trial—the Senate imposed restrictions that ranged from the petty, refusing to let the managers use an overhead projector to present certain evidence, to the basic, limiting the managers to three witnesses, each of whom could only be questioned on videotape, not in person on the Senate floor—Hyde had been too courteous.

"It might have been appropriate," Hyde explained, "for me to stand up and say, 'Gentlemen, in a fair trial, we ought to be able to present our case. We can't. We're hog-tied. I don't think that's what the Constitution envisioned.' I never said anything like that. I just bowed gracefully from the waist and took what they gave us."

If Henry Hyde had been bitter, I wouldn't have been surprised. Starr had forced Hyde to hold hearings only on Monica. The Senate had made it impossible for him to stage a trial. James Carville and other Clinton operatives had spent months reviling him. Cranks had threatened his life. The press had dug up an affair he had had three decades before, humiliating him. I kept expecting Hyde to avail himself of a standard technique of politicians, waving at me to turn off my tape recorder, then, safely off the record, savaging his enemies. Instead Hyde remained on the record, self-effacing and affable, refusing to speak ill of anyone but himself. Only once did his equanimity desert him. Even then he expressed not anger but bewilderment. For the life of him, Hyde said, he couldn't understand why the American people had responded to the impeachment proceedings as they had.

Hyde explained that he had never expected the Senate to convict the president. "But I was always of the mind that if the American people could hear the story in a coherent way, putting all the pieces together, they would become as revulsed at this situation as we [the House managers] were. That never happened." Even though the Senate blocked a full trial, the House managers made it clear that the president had obstructed justice, lying under oath and tampering with witnesses. "But the poll figures never moved," Hyde said.

"Did that shake your confidence in the American people?" I asked.

"Yes it did," Hyde said. He took a long, thoughtful draw on his cigar. "What is the explanation? A lack of community concern? People saying to themselves, 'My job is okay, the unemployment rate is down, interest rates are down, inflation is down?' " Hyde looked troubled. "I don't know. I just don't know. I'm still trying to figure it out."

It now looks as though the impeachment proceedings may have helped Republicans after all—the American people didn't want Bill Clinton removed from office, but they came to hold the Clinton administration in such low regard that they don't particularly want Al Gore to succeed Bill Clinton, either. Yet the House Republicans remain dazed by the impeachment proceedings all the same. Bill Clinton was the one who had a tawdry affair with a woman young enough to be his daughter, then obstructed justice to hide it. The House Republicans were the ones whose poll ratings fell. How could that have happened? If instead of pursuing a Republican agenda with zest and self-confidence the House Republicans find themselves scratching their heads, dazed and uncertain, they may perhaps be forgiven. They're still trying to figure it out.

THE MANAGING PARTNER

Congressman Christopher Cox of California and I got to know each other when we worked at opposite ends of a hallway in the Reagan White House. Chris, who holds a degree from Harvard Law School, was a member of the counsel's office. One of his duties was to prevent unauthorized use of the presidential seal.

"It's mostly little mom-and-pop outfits that misuse the seal," Chris explained to me in his White House office one afternoon. He pulled open a drawer of his desk. Inside lay a heap of glass paperweights with the presidential seal engraved on the bottom, dinner plates with the presidential seal painted in the middle, and cellophane bags of stale peanuts with the presidential seal stamped on the side of each bag.

"How do you get the people who make this stuff to stop?" I asked.

"I write them a letter on White House stationery, telling them to cease and desist or face the full prosecutorial powers of the United States government." Chris broke into a grin. "I like getting things done."

First elected to the House in 1988, just months after leaving the Reagan administration, Chris has demonstrated the same zest for getting things done as a member of Congress that he demonstrated as a member of the White House staff. Still trim and handsome he has authored a dozen important pieces of legislation, including one of the only two bills ever enacted over President Clinton's veto, the 1995 Securities Litigation Reform Act. He has climbed into the ranks of the House leadership, serving as chairman of the House Policy Committee, a capacity in which he helps to establish the agenda for the entire Republican caucus. He chaired the select committee that investigated allegations of Chinese spying. In 1999, after nearly a year of work, Chris's committee produced a three-volume report, which quickly became known as the Cox Report, concluding that the Chinese did indeed steal American nuclear secrets, leaping from 1950s-style nuclear weapons to 1990s-style nuclear weapons on the basis of what they learned, and that the Clinton administration let them get away with it. In recent months, Chris has authored proposals to rein in trial lawyers and to keep the Internet free of taxes.

Given all that Chris had achieved in Congress, when I visited him on Capitol Hill I expected him to speak of the institution with pride. Instead he spoke about it with frustration. "Congress is a two-centuries-old bureaucracy. As everyone knows, the founders designed Congress with a lot of checks and balances to make sure that not a lot got done very fast." Chris shook his head. "It worked. Not a lot *does* get done very fast."

Chris offered the Cox Report as a case in point. When he was appointed chairman of the select committee that published the report, Chris knew that some of the committee's findings would probably reflect badly on the Clinton administration. Chris therefore decided that he wanted the committee to be able to publish its report unanimously, without as much as a single dissent from any of its members, demonstrating that the report had the support of the committee's four Democrats as well as its five Republicans. To produce a unanimous report, in turn, Chris decided that he had to avoid holding hearings in public. Now, public hearings represent a revered congressional tradition. Yet Chris was convinced that the members of his committee would find it impossible to resist partisan posturing once television cameras had been permitted into the committee room. Chris got lucky. Since much of the material the committee would be dealing with was classified, it soon became clear that the committee was going to have to hold many of its meetings in secret in any event. Chris was able to persuade the other members of the committee to hold the remainder of their meetings in secret as well. "There was a dividend to dealing with classified material," he said.

Even after sidestepping one of the most cumbersome aspects of congressional procedure, public hearings, Chris found that he still had to spend the next six months, the period during which the select committee conducted its investigations, working twelve to sixteen hours a day. "I put everything on hold, all the way up to and including a lot of family things. I was an absentee dad for a lot of this period of time," Chris explained. When the three-volume Cox Report was finally published, every member of the select committee did indeed support it, making it one of the few unanimous and bipartisan committee reports that the House of Representatives has ever produced. Yet the work left Chris exhausted. "It was just a huge effort," he said. "Huge."

"At least it must have given you a sense of satisfaction," I suggested. " 'The Cox Report.' Not many people get that kind of billing."

Chris smiled sadly, as if he were dealing with an idiot child. After all that the press had done to the Cox Report, he explained, he almost wished that his name had never been associated with it.

Chris stood from the sofa to walk to his desk. He picked up a newspaper clipping. "This is an editorial from the *Minneapolis Star-Tribune*," Chris said. He skimmed the clipping, searching for a particular sentence. "Here it is," he said. "Listen to this. 'The report is subtly but palpably partisan.'"

"Partisan?" Chris said, exasperated. He tossed the clipping back onto his desk. " 'Partisan' is exactly what the report is *not*. It's *completely* bipartisan. But since they didn't like what the report said, they ignored the facts and called it 'partisan' anyway."

The newspaper that galled Chris the most was the *Los Angeles Times*, partly because it was the dominant newspaper in his region of the country, Southern California, partly because he had gone to the trouble of driving to Los Angeles to meet the newspaper's editorial board not long before the Cox Report was published. The editors of the *Los Angeles Times* knew, because Chris had told them so himself, that the Cox Report was completely bipartisan, based on meticulous research, and intended only to report on the theft of American nuclear secrets, not to demean any ethnic group. The *Los Angeles Times* had nevertheless run one story after another suggesting that the Cox Report was racist. "These people have *so* screwed me," Chris said. "I mean, you're taping this, and I don't want to sound paranoid. But if we can't go after a few spies without being accused of being anti-Chinese, I mean, I just don't know how all of this is supposed to work."

Listening to Chris, I thought back to a conversation I had had with David Brady. In David's view Republicans seldom felt as much at home in the House of Representatives as did Democrats. He named two reasons for the Republicans' discomfort. The first was the nature of the work itself.

"Democrats like the process for its own sake," David argued. "What Republicans like is getting things done. To them, the process just gets in the way.

"Turn on C-Span and watch a hearing sometime," David said. When the camera pans to the Democratic side, you'll see congressmen who were enjoying themselves. They'd be passing notes back and forth to their staffs. They'd be exchanging whispered asides and chuckling. But when the camera pans to the Republican side, you'll see a different picture.

"You watch them," David said. "The Republicans will all have their chins in their hands and a glassy look in their eyes. They'll be wondering why they ran for Congress in the first place." Calling witnesses, raising points of order, posturing for television cameras, holding votes—Democrats tend to thrive on it, Republicans to see it as claptrap.

Christopher Cox bore David out, disliking congressional claptrap so much that, as we have seen, he had avoided holding any public hearings at all.

The second reason Republicans seldom felt as much at home in the House as did Democrats, David believed, was that it cost Republicans so much to be there. David told me about the Lincoln Club of Northern California. Made up mostly of businesspeople, the Lincoln Club recruits Republicans to run for office, giving them financial backing. "Do you have any idea how hard it is for the Lincoln Club to find people to run for Congress?" David asked. "They have to beg—literally beg."

When the Lincoln Club found an executive who was Republican, well-spoken, and interested in public policy, it would send several of its members to his office. Attempting to persuade this capable, intelligent individual to abandon his career in business, they would explain that if he won his race for Congress he would earn a congressional salary of $136,700 a year. The reaction of the executive was nearly always the same. For a moment he would look at them. Then he would burst out laughing. The Lincoln Club had acquired a considerable reputation as a local source of merriment.

The Lincoln Club's Democratic counterpart, a group of businesspeople who, like the members of the Lincoln Club, provide candidates with financial backing, found itself facing the opposite problem, not too few candidates for Congress but too many. "We're talking social workers, schoolteachers, public defenders, associate pastors of Unitarian churches— professional do-gooders," David said. "Every election cycle there are dozens of them, all desperate to run for Congress as Democrats. For people like that, getting into Congress would be a big step up." Democrats in Silicon Valley had to interview one prospect after another before they could even begin to winnow the list.

Of course Silicon Valley represents an extreme. "You haven't got middle-level talent pulling down the big bucks in Kansas that middle-level talent pulls down out there," David said. But the GOP faces the same problem throughout the country even so. The owner of a car dealership in Topeka, the surgeon in Moline, the McDonald's franchisee in Mason City— to serve in Congress, each would have to accept a pay cut.

"At least on the Senate side you get a little prestige out of the job," David said. "But Republicans in the House? It's only one voter in five who can even *name* his member of Congress."

Here, too, Christopher Cox bore David out. After all, he had been elected to Congress as a man in his middle thirties, just entering his prime. He had now spent a dozen of the most dazzling years in the history of the American economy on a government paycheck. If instead of going home to Southern California to run for Congress he had gone home to join a law firm (when we worked at the White House, I always pictured Chris as the managing partner of a major firm), his income would have been—well, you get the idea. Chris certainly did. His face sank as I asked him about it.

"I have to say that I've asked myself that many times," Chris replied. It wasn't as if he derived no satisfaction from serving in the House, Chris explained. He was proud of the legislation he had authored. He was certain the Cox Report had made the nation more secure. But make the House his entire career? Forgo the private sector entirely? The income? The ability to get things done, unencumbered by politics? "If I died tomorrow and it were my epitaph that I had been a member of Congress, I'd feel horrible about it. I'd be dead, of course, so I'm not sure what I'd feel. But you see what I mean."

Indeed I did. Any Republican would.

Not long after I left Washington, D.C., Republicans in the House of Representatives managed to pass a ten-year, $800 billion tax cut. Speaker Denny Hastert trumpeted the tax cut as a historic achievement, and for a while I thought I was going to have to take back everything I had written in my notes about the dazed mien of the House Republicans. I needn't have worried.

When the Republican tax cut reached the president he vetoed it, claiming the cut was so big that it would have returned us to the days of massive federal deficits. By then Republican budget experts outside Congress had had time to study the measure. They learned that over the first several years it would have cut taxes scarcely at all. When the measure finally did begin cutting taxes, the tax cuts would have been modest—and contingent on the ability of the economy to provide the federal government with revenues at certain prescribed rates. While the president was denouncing the House Republicans for their rashness, knowledgeable Republicans were thus denouncing the House Republicans for their timidity. The tax cuts, intended to demonstrate that the House Republicans still had an agenda, demonstrated only their fecklessness instead.

Now, you would think that if Republicans in the House have become feckless, Republican governors and mayors would have done the same. They haven't. While over the past several years Republicans in the House have accomplished little but the impeachment of the president, Republican governors and mayors have produced a remarkable string of accomplishments. Governor Tommy Thompson of Wisconsin has instituted sweeping welfare reforms. Governors George Pataki of New York, Tom Ridge of Pennsylvania, John Engler of Michigan, and others have cut taxes. Mayor Richard Riordan of Los Angeles has overseen improvements in his city's schools. Mayor Rudolph Giuliani of New York has presided over a drop in the crime rate that has helped to make New York, still a dangerous metropolis when Giuliani took office, into the safest large city in the country. Republican governors and mayors seem to have a knack for getting things done. To find out why, I visited Bret Schundler, the mayor of Jersey City, who has compiled one of the most impressive records of any Republican in the nation.

RICH MAN, POOR CITY

To prepare for my interview with Mayor Schundler, I looked over Jersey City's Web site. One item in particular arrested my attention: Mayor Schundler's second inaugural address. It was unlike the remarks of any politician I had ever seen. The address wasn't folksy. It made no attempt to establish a rapport between the speaker and his audience. It offered no particular call to action. Instead it laid out the mayor's governing philosophy, delving into the history of the Middle Ages, the Renaissance, and the Enlightenment, and quoting Jean-Jacques Rousseau, Immanuel Kant, and Friedrich Nietzsche. Running to several thousand words, the address read like a lecture at a divinity school, and the fourth time I found the mayor quoting Nietzsche I began to wonder whether someone in his audience might have considered circulating a recall petition just to get him to stop speaking. Yet in a city that is more than half black and Hispanic, with a total Republican registration a minuscule 9 percent, Bret Schundler, a white man from the suburbs who likes to give long, earnest speeches, has been elected mayor three times.

Walking around Jersey City before meeting Bret Schundler, I found one block on Grove Street that shows how the city looked before Schundler became mayor. A decade ago a developer made a bid for the properties on the west side of the block (the east side is occupied by city hall). Then the developer ran into financial trouble, tying the properties up in legal proceedings ever since. The properties are dilapidated buildings of brownstone and brick. At ground level several of the buildings contain small businesses—Grove Liquor and Deli, Olympic Cleaners, Tangles Hair Studio, Carlascio Orthopedic ("Prosthetics, Orthotics, and Footwear Prescriptions Filled"). Above ground level, however, most of the buildings are unoccupied, their windows smashed or boarded over. A scant decade ago all of Jersey City was just like this—derelict and half deserted.

Jersey City still isn't a garden spot, but it is visibly a city that works. On the blocks surrounding the dilapidated buildings, I found well-maintained grocery stores, drugstores, and restaurants lining every street. The upper stories of buildings were occupied, curtains fluttering in the windows. The sidewalks were crowded with African-Americans, Hispanics, Indians, and Pakistanis, all of whom seemed at ease in each other's company and all of whom walked purposefully, like people with jobs. The long economic boom of the 1990s of course played a role in Jersey City's revival. But if the economy were entirely responsible, then nearby towns should have changed for the better just as dramatically. They haven't. The difference is Mayor Schundler.

Schundler, 41, works in a small office on the second floor of city hall. His office has a vault built into the wall. "The mayor's office used to be on the other side of the building," Schundler explained with a smile. "Then one of my predecessors realized it would make his life simpler if he just worked next to the money." In 1991, Mayor Gerald McCann, who controlled Jersey City's Democratic machine, was convicted of defrauding a Florida savings and loan. Three months later, in 1992, a New Jersey Supreme Court ruling forced McCann from office. Schundler won the special election that followed. He immediately embarked on half a dozen initiatives, first using skills he had learned on Wall Street to monetize the city's tax receipts, bringing in desperately needed cash. His most dramatic initiative involved city hall itself. A large, handsome granite building dedicated in 1896, city hall had been one of the proudest structures in Jersey City until 1979, when a fire burned out the roof. The government of Jersey City then did just what residents of burned-out homes throughout Jersey City had gotten into the habit of doing— it had learned to live in a decaying hulk. Schundler renovated city hall, rebuilding the roof and cleaning the place up. It was his way of letting people know that Jersey City was going to become a self-respecting municipality again.

Schundler grew up in Westfield, a middle-class, suburban New Jersey town, one of nine children whose father made an impression on all of them. "My father would say, 'Of him to whom much has been given, much is expected,' " Schundler told me. "He would ask us questions at the dinner table. 'The middle class has moved out of New York City. Is that good or bad?' 'There's litter on the streets. What can be done about it?' He was always pushing us for ways to make the world a little bit better."

For all his high-mindedness, Schundler is relaxed and engaging. He has bright eyes set in a face that, even though his sandy hair is already flecked with gray, is round enough to make him look younger than he is. He smiles easily. He laughs a lot. Even when he is talking about his aspirations for making the world better, which he does constantly, it is a pleasure listening to him.

Schundler obtained his first exposure to politics after graduating from Harvard. Convinced that he wanted to become an urban minister, he moved to Washington, D.C., to write a thesis about an inner-city church. A Democrat—he believed that Democrats cared more about the poor than did Republicans—Schundler found that he had enough free time to take a job in the office of a Democratic congressman. On Capitol Hill he met people close to Senator Gary Hart, and soon

Schundler moved to Iowa as a volunteer on Hart's 1984 presidential campaign.

Schundler found Hart disappointing. While the candidate's elevated ideals may have looked admirable to people outside the campaign, to people inside the campaign they looked arrogant. "We were there, sacrificing like crazy, working like dogs," Schundler said. "But Hart had the sense that all he was going to do was think of some good ideas, and it would be up to everybody else to achieve them. We'd ask him to sit on a bale of hay for a photo op. He wouldn't do it. We'd ask him to call up a contributor to say thank you. He wouldn't do it. If you're going to move the country forward, it's worth paying some price."

(When photographs of Hart frolicking on a cabin cruiser with a young woman were published four years later, during Hart's 1988 presidential campaign, the incident struck Schundler as merely one more example of Hart's self-indulgence. "Our call is to try to think about others and make this a better society. If you're going to accept that responsibility, it's going to involve some sacrifice. Some men died in battle for a better world. All Hart had to do was remain faithful to his wife.")

When Hart lost the 1984 Democratic nomination to Walter Mondale, a politician that Schundler considered in thrall to the unions, Schundler was left without a candidate. Wondering whom to support, he found himself listening to the speeches of the presidential candidate he had heretofore ignored, Ronald Reagan.

Schundler still believed that Republicans cared only about the haves, not about the have-nots. Yet Schundler noticed a strain in Reagan's message that he found appealing. "Reagan gave people a sense of personal responsibility," Schundler said. "I believe in telling people they have not just the ability but the *obligation* to overcome the obstacles in their lives. If you sit around and wallow in self-pity, you're going to be perfectly useless to others. Reagan was communicating that message."

Disheartened with Democratic politics and broke after paying his own expenses while he volunteered for Gary Hart, Schundler sat down with a pen and a pad of paper to think about what he wanted to do next. After listing the characteristics he wanted in a job, including "something that keeps me in touch with what's happening in the world," "being entrepreneurial," and "working with sharp people," Schundler decided to go into the securities industry. An intelligent, ambitious young man, Schundler joined Salomon Brothers in 1984, landing on Wall Street at the precise moment when intelligent, ambitious young men could make more money than ever before. In 1987 Schundler left Salomon Brothers for C. J. Lawrence Securities, to switch from selling bonds, which he found boring and lucrative, to selling equities, which he found fascinating and lucrative. In 1990, with millions of dollars in the bank, Schundler retired. He was thirty.

During his brief Wall Street career, Schundler and his wife had lived in Jersey City. They had done so for the sake of convenience. From Jersey City, Schundler's wife had an easy commute across Newark Bay to Newark proper, where she was attending law school, while Schundler himself had an easy commute across the Hudson River to Wall Street. Yet Schundler had soon made the derelict city the object of his altruistic impulses. He helped to operate a food pantry at the Old Bergen Church and became president of the Downtown Coalition of Neighborhood Associations. Thus when Mayor

McCann was indicted in 1991, Schundler found the prospect of running for mayor himself irresistible.

Before entering the race, Schundler had one matter to tidy up. He was still a registered Democrat. In a city in which more than 80 percent of the voters were themselves registered Democrats this hardly placed Schundler at a disadvantage. Yet some time ago—he couldn't say just when—he had recognized that on the big issues the Republicans were right. Cutting taxes really did promote economic growth. Economic growth really did mean more jobs for everybody, including the poor. "It was guys like Jack Kemp and Newt Gingrich who were talking about rolling up our sleeves and actually trying to address poverty," Schundler explained. The Republican registration of Jersey City was then just 6 percent, even lower than today's 9 percent. But if he was going to be honest with Jersey City's voters, Schundler had no choice but to change his registration. He did so, ran for mayor as a Republican—and, to his surprise, won.

Schundler has replaced a political machine with a municipal government of utter rectitude. He has expanded the tax base, presiding over a project in which half a dozen attractive new skyscrapers have gone up on the edge of the Hudson, thereby expanding the waterfront's share of Jersey City's tax revenues from a tiny portion to 30 percent. He has cut taxes and reduced the welfare rolls. He has established good relations between the police and the populace—Schundler presides over a city, indeed, that appears to be positively glowing with good race relations. One reason is that the mayor has used tax revenues from the waterfront, which is largely white, to redevelop Martin Luther King Boulevard, which is almost entirely black. Twenty blocks of abandoned buildings when Schundler took office, today Martin Luther King Plaza is the center of a thriving neighborhood with a new super-market, new restaurants, a new auto supply store. "And all these are African-American-owned businesses," Schundler told me proudly.

Schundler has even addressed Jersey City's spiritual life. Originally pro-choice, after taking office Schundler became pro-life. "I used to believe that fetuses weren't human be-cause we'd all *feel* worse if we were actually taking human lives. Then a friend said, 'People had a way of defining away the humanity of African-Americans during the Civil War. Feel-ings are cultural constructs. You shouldn't let them be a guide to what is moral or not.' " While Schundler was thinking over the best way to express his new pro-life conviction, the san-itation department found a dead baby in the sewage system. "You'd be surprised how many bodies turn up in a city like this," Schundler said. "Lots of times, no one can identify them." In a public ceremony, Schundler joined the city's min-isters, priests, rabbis, and Islamic clerics in dedicating a memorial to all those in Jersey City who die forgotten or un-known.

How has Schundler compiled such a remarkable list of achievements? The answer is simple. He saw what needed to be done—really, when you listen to him, you come to be-lieve that all it took was a man of goodwill with a decent head on his shoulders—and he *did* it. Of course, he had to win approval for each of his initiatives from his city coun-cil. But that never proved much of an obstacle. He was the mayor. The city council *expected* him to lead. How different is the life of a Republican who finds himself as an execu-tive from the life of a Republican who finds himself merely one of the 435 members of the House of Representatives.

I asked Schundler what he would do after stepping down

as mayor. It had crossed my mind that he might run for the House. "I'm planning on running for governor of New Jersey in 2001," Schundler replied. Governor. An executive position, not a legislative one. Of course.

Washington, D.C., and Jersey City, New Jersey. In one city, a couple of hundred Republican legislators list haplessly along, frustrated and anxious, unable to see what difference their careers might be making to anyone. No doubt they have prevented the Clinton administration from raising taxes and making the government bigger. But it is difficult to feel much sense of accomplishment when your principal achievement is keeping the government gridlocked. In the other city, a Republican mayor, self-confident and energetic, enacts one initiative after another, producing palpable improvements in the lives of virtually every citizen in his city. It is worth noting that while Washington has a press corps of thousands, Jersey City has a press corps of none (to the extent that coverage of Mayor Schundler appears anywhere, it appears in the *Trenton Times*). The ramifications of this disparity in press coverage are obvious—and, for the GOP, baleful. Republicans in Congress affect the way Americans see the GOP far more than Mayor Schundler—or any mayor or governor, since the coverage such figures receive is nearly always limited to their own cities and states—ever can.

The next time you turn on the television and see a House Republican looking bewildered or grim or forlorn, force yourself to remember this: Somewhere in America there is a Republican governor or mayor who is smiling.

Chapter Seven

THE PRICKLY LADIES OF THE CACTUS STATE, OR WOMEN

Journal entry:

I still don't know why Edita had to get so testy about it. I was only conducting a mental experiment. The trouble is, the more I thought about it, the more intrigued I became. If women had never been given the vote, just how different would *the country look?*

The Nineteenth Amendment to the Constitution, which in 1920 gave women the vote, was one of four amendments enacted during the second decade of the twentieth century. The other three proved dubious. The Sixteenth Amendment, enacted in 1913, gave the federal government the right to levy income taxes. The government quickly used that right to gain control over the entire economy. The Seventeenth Amendment, also enacted in 1913, denied state legislatures the right to elect United States senators, mandating the popular election of senators instead. The amendment thereby undermined states' rights. The Eighteenth Amendment, enacted in 1919, decreed prohibition. Prohibition? Enough said.

"Maybe the Nineteenth Amendment was just part of a

bad streak," I said to Edita. "I mean, it's not as if giving women the vote was inevitable. In Switzerland, one canton denied women the vote until 1989, another until 1991. The cantons only gave in when the rest of Switzerland decided to make a stink about it.

"Imagine it," I continued. "An America run entirely by guys. Lower taxes. Complete laissez-faire for business. Just about the only government items would be bond issues to build sports stadiums."

Edita looked at me. "I'm giving you one chance to tell me you're not serious," she said.

"I wasn't serious at first. Now I'm not so sure."

She stood.

"You don't have to get offended," I said. "Where's your sense of humor, anyway?"

She walked out of the room.

"Hey!" I called after her. "Who's making dinner?"

W hen I mentioned the gender gap to Newt Gingrich, his temper flared. "If Republicans get the votes of fewer women than men, then it's a simple mathematical fact that Democrats get the votes of fewer men than women. Why doesn't the press ask the Democrats about *their* gender gap?" he said.

Gingrich had a point. Yet whether or not the press harps on the Democratic gender gap, the Republican gender gap still exists. Indeed, it existed for twenty years before the press began to write about it during President Reagan's 1984 re-election campaign. Studies indicate that with one exception, the election of 1976, when Gerald Ford won 49 percent of the votes of both genders, the Republican candidate has won the votes of fewer women than men in each of the nine presidential elections since 1964. In six of the nine, the elections of 1972, 1980, 1984, 1988, 1992, and 1996, the Republican candidate received only nine or fewer votes from women for every ten votes he received from men. In at least one election (the election of 1996) the gender gap cost the GOP the White House: If Bob Dole had received the same proportion of the women's vote that he received of the men's vote, he would have become president. Bob Dole as president. Now there's a thought to cheer you.

I set out to learn what caused the gender gap. Once I had the answer to that question, I reasoned, I'd be able to figure out how Republicans could close it. This leg of my journey across the Republican landscape proved less straightforward than I expected.

"I call them YDWs," Jack told me. "Young dumb women."

Jack is a political consultant. He has devoted himself to getting Republicans elected to state legislatures. Part of the reason is that Jack likes the challenge. The other part is that so few other GOP political consultants care to compete with him for the business. As a general rule, the higher the office, the easier it has proven for Republicans to win. If you think of holding office as eating a pie, then since the Second World War the GOP has eaten about half the presidential pie, about three sevenths of the gubernatorial pie, and about two fifths of the congressional pie. But it has eaten only slivers of the state legislative pie. Even today, when the GOP controls both houses of Congress and occupies thirty of the fifty governors' mansions, it controls only thirty-two of the nation's ninety-nine state legislative chambers (each of the fifty states has two legislative chambers except Nebraska, which has only one). Since so many of his own clients end up losing, Jack has become an expert on the forces that defeat Republicans. The gender gap is one of them. Jack's explanation for the gender gap is elegant in its sweeping simplicity: There are a lot of women out there who actually believe what they see on *Oprah.*

Jack eyed my tape recorder. "You've got to be careful how you use what I tell you," Jack said. "I mean, it's all true. YDWs vote against us all the time. But talking about it could get me in trouble. Political correctness and all." It was then that I decided to write about him under the name of "Jack" instead of his real name.

Why are there only YDWs, young dumb women, and no YDMs, young dumb men? "Men are skeptical," Jack explained. "Women aren't." Men are taught to figure things out for themselves from an early age. Women are taught to be passive. They'll permit others to figure things out for them.

"Why won't a man stop to ask for directions?" Jack asked. "Because he's a man. He's supposed to find his way on his own. But women? If that's the way a complete stranger tells them to go, they'll drive a hundred miles in the wrong direction and then go over a cliff."

Just as they permit themselves to be told where to drive, YDWs permit themselves to be told what politics to adopt. No one comes right out and tells them to vote Democratic in so many words. The message that YDWs receive is much more subtle than that. But it amounts to the same thing. "We're talking about women who want a little glamour in their lives," Jack said. YDWs thus seek to emulate the people they see on television and in magazines. They copy their hairstyles.

They imitate their wardrobes. And they conform to their politics. "Oprah doesn't go strutting her politics around on her TV show," Jack said. "But everybody knows without having to be told that Oprah's no Republican. Next time you go to the grocery store, look at the magazines for sale at the checkout counter. The whole YDW culture is right there."

Jack is a political professional. If he said a lot of women were YDWs, I supposed, then maybe they were. And my next trip to the grocery store seemed to bear him out. While the cashier rang up my purchases, I picked up a copy of *People*. My eye fell on "Cause Celebs," a story about Hollywood stars who had visited Washington to lobby Congress. Ted Danson wanted new laws to protect beaches. Anthony Edwards was seeking more money for research on autism, David Hyde-Pierce for research on Alzheimer's. Andie MacDowell intended to block the construction of a pipeline in Montana. I closed my eyes, trying to see stars lobbying for conservative causes. Andie MacDowell pushing for tax cuts? Ted Danson seeking tort reform? To state the case is to declare its absurdity. If Jack wanted to contend that the pop culture of which *People* is a part serves as a transmission belt, conveying liberal politics from Hollywood to American women, then I couldn't gainsay him.

But Jack's explanation of the gender gap still bothered me. If women were as dumb as he argued, then giving them the vote had been a mistake. Yet back in 1920, it had been Republicans who pushed the Nineteenth Amendment through the Senate. Had the GOP been right to free the slaves but wrong to enfranchise women?

THE PRICKLY LADIES OF THE CACTUS STATE

Not long after speaking with Jack, I happened to hear a speech by Senator John McCain. In passing, McCain claimed that most of the top positions in the government of Arizona, his home state, were held by Republican women. I looked into it. McCain was right. Of the five offices in Arizona that are filled by statewide elections—governor, secretary of state, treasurer, attorney general, and superintendent of schools—all five are held by women, while the senior-most position in the legislature, president of the senate, is held by a woman, too. Of the six, only one, the attorney general, is a Democrat. The rest are all Republicans.

I flew to Phoenix. I felt sure the women who run Arizona had the gender gap all figured out.

Betsey Bayless, the first of the four Republican women with whom I spoke, is the Arizona secretary of state. As such, she is responsible for conducting elections, registering trade names and trademarks, and other administrative tasks. Arizona secretary of state isn't a position people grow up burning with ambition to hold—I myself had to check her Web site to find out what she did—but Bayless oversees a budget of $6 million and a staff of thirty-six. And since Arizona lacks a lieutenant governor, she is next in line to the governor. This amounts to more than a constitutional nicety. In recent years scandals have forced two men to vacate the office of governor, which was then filled by two different secretaries of state, in both cases, as it happened, a woman.

Bayless, in her mid-fifties, is attractive and poised. We sat at a table in her office on the seventh floor of the executive building, immediately behind the state capitol. Her window looked north toward the glass towers of downtown Phoenix, showing skyscrapers glinting in the sun. Bayless had her secretary bring us each a cup of coffee. Then we began talking about how Bayless got where she was.

Bayless knew from an early age that she wanted to work for a living, she explained. When she graduated from the University of Tucson in 1964 with a degree in international banking, she was determined to get a job with one of Arizona's banks, which were doing more and more business with Latin America. She pictured herself drumming up business, devising new ways of financing international trade, doing deals. Then she interviewed at every bank of any size in the entire state. The best offer she got was for a job overseeing file clerks. She gritted her teeth and took it. Although her duties bored her, Bayless performed them well, deciding that sooner or later her diligence would be rewarded with a job in banking, not filing. Then one day her supervisor took her aside. Her diligence had indeed been noticed—but it was going to be rewarded with candid advice, not a promotion. The supervisor told Bayless that because she was a woman, she would never be able to escape the clerical department no matter how hard she worked. "You're too talented," he told her. "Leave. Leave or you'll be stuck here your entire career."

"At that point I did a review of the working world," Bayless said. She surveyed one industry after another—retail, insurance, real estate. In none did women hold responsible positions. Then she looked into state government. There women had risen into management. The explanation? "The top male graduates weren't seeking government work," Bayless said. "They all ran off to real estate and banking, where the action was."

Bayless went back to school, earned a degree in public

policy, then got a job with the state and began working her way up. Over the years she compiled a remarkable series of firsts. She became the first woman to head a state agency, the first woman to sit in a governor's cabinet, and the first woman to chair a governor's cabinet. In 1987, Bayless left the state government to become a banker, finally realizing her original ambition. Then, in 1989, when a vacancy occurred on the Maricopa County Board of Supervisors, Bayless was appointed to fill it. The job proved a big one—Maricopa County, in which Phoenix is located, contains almost 60 percent of the population of the state. So in 1997, when Governor Jane Dee Hull offered to appoint Bayless to complete Hull's own unexpired term as Arizona secretary of state— Hull was one of the secretaries of state who became governor when her predecessor as governor resigned—Bayless felt qualified to accept. In 1998 Bayless was elected to a term as Arizona secretary of state in her own right.

I noticed an odd aspect of Bayless's tale. Although she had been a Republican all her life, for much of her career her fellow Republicans hadn't helped her. If anything they had stood in her way. A Democratic governor, Bruce Babbitt, had given Bayless her biggest promotions, naming her to head the Department of Public Administration, then inviting her to chair his cabinet. Then a Republican governor, Evan Mecham, who would become famous for rescinding Martin Luther King Jr. Day as a state holiday, refused to appoint Bayless to a senior position in his administration. "He also made it pretty clear he didn't think much of women in responsible positions in the first place," Bayless said. It was after Mecham became governor that Bayless left state government.

After treatment like that, why had Bayless even remained a Republican? Bayless smiled knowingly. It was clearly a question to which she had given some thought. "Believe me," she said, "my political life would have been a lot easier if I had been a Democrat, and I was given lots of chances to change parties and become one. But I just couldn't leave the Republican Party. I believe in people taking responsibility for their own lives."

Now that Bayless had told me her story, it was time to raise the subject of gender politics. I tossed her a softball of a question, inquiring about the 1998 election in which Bayless and the other women now running Arizona had been elected. How had this triumph for women come about? Instead of taking a swing at the question, Bayless let it land with a thud.

"All of the women were known commodities," she replied flatly. "They'd all had a lot of experience. It wasn't all that surprising they were elected."

That was it. I tried again, pitching Bayless another easy one. Of course the candidates had a lot of experience, I said. But a band of sisters had grasped hands, then burst through the glass ceiling. Didn't she see that as a remarkable accomplishment?

Bayless let this question, too, land with a thud. "The gender thing was remarked on after the election," she said. "Before the election, it wasn't. It wasn't a factor. Not to the voters—and not to us."

Without thinking about it, I realized, I had taken it for granted that Bayless would follow one of two scripts. In the first script, she would have championed the GOP as a vehicle for women's progress. "It's no accident that nearly all the women elected in 1998 were Republicans," Bayless would have said. "The GOP is breaking down barriers for women at every level. Republican women are on the march." In the second script, Bayless would have given vent to feminist frustrations with the GOP. "The way the Republican Party has treated women is outrageous," Bayless would have said. "The GOP should drop the pro-life plank from its platform. It should drop its support for guns. It should embrace affirmative action for women. And now that I'm a high official, I intend to do all I can to see that the GOP does just that."

But both scripts would have dealt with women as a class, not as individuals. Bayless herself didn't see women that way. She had just told me that she was a Republican because she believed in individual responsibility. She had succeeded in her own struggle because she had taken charge of her life, worked hard, and asked to be judged only on her merits. Now here she was, the second-ranking official in the entire state of Arizona. I could toss her all the softball questions about gender politics that I wanted. Betsey Bayless wouldn't play.

When I asked about the GOP's support for guns, Bayless shrugged. In Arizona, she explained, guns weren't much of an issue because westerners felt so comfortable with them. "Even women?" I pressed. Bayless smiled. "Women can use guns, too," she said. When I asked about abortion, Bayless replied that her own position was in the middle. She disliked abortion. But she couldn't see permitting the government to ban it. "Arizona already has a law that makes partial birth abortions illegal," Bayless said. "I think that makes sense. I think most women do, too." Would it help the GOP appeal to women if it dropped the pro-life plank from its platform? "The Republican Party is a great big party," Bayless replied. "There's plenty of room for different views."

Leaving Bayless's office, I found myself wondering how I was going to justify the cost of my flight to Phoenix. I had come to the high desert to get a woman's view of the Republican Party. When I got it, I couldn't tell it apart from a man's.

Next I went downstairs to the office of the state treasurer, Carol Springer. Springer is a gal. If Phoenix had been Dodge City, she would have been Miss Kitty. In her early sixties, she has blond hair piled high on her head, high cheekbones, and a look that lets you know that while you're talking she's sizing you up.

Springer moved to Phoenix from Oregon thirty years ago. Shortly thereafter, her husband walked out on her, leaving her to raise their five children. Deciding that it would be easier to keep an eye on her brood in a small town, Springer moved to Prescott, about eighty miles north of Phoenix, where the principal industries were ranching and mining (Prescott has since become a center of high tech). Springer supported her family as a real estate agent. "I raised those children on my own," Springer, seated at her desk, told me. "I've been independent a long time now."

In 1990 Springer ran for the Arizona senate. She didn't want to. The man who already represented Prescott in the senate was a friend. But the economy was, as she put it, "in the pits," and when the legislature enacted a tax hike, her friend, the Prescott senator, cast the deciding vote. "If you want to help the economy," Springer said, disgusted, "you don't raise taxes. That's just logic." Springer tried to get someone else to run against her friend. When no one would, she reluctantly decided to announce against him herself. All she wanted to do was send her friend the message that he ought to think twice before voting for any more tax hikes. He refused to take her seriously. "When I called him up to tell him I was running, he just laughed and laughed," Springer said.

That left her with no choice. She had to wage a campaign. "I had no money. I never held a fund-raiser. All I talked about was that one issue, taxes." Springer won by two hundred out of eighteen thousand votes. "On election night," she said, "the two most surprised people were my opponent and me."

Springer served in the Arizona senate eight years. The GOP controlled the body for six of those years, allowing Springer and her fellow Republicans to win the passage of nearly all the legislation they wanted. They enacted charter school legislation. They reformed the state welfare system. They reformed the entire state budget process. Springer enjoyed the senate just as long as she and her fellow Republicans were getting things done. But when Arizona's Republicans seemed to lose their sense of initiative—at just about the same time, as it happened, that Republicans in Washington lost theirs—Springer grew impatient. "During the Contract with America time we had real goals. But now it's like we're just kind of going along."

Bored with the senate, Springer decided to run for state treasurer. She knew she would have less influence over policy than she had in the senate. But in reforming the state budget process she had learned the ins and outs of state finances, and she believed she would enjoy the work.

Like Betsey Bayless, Carol Springer thus had an impressive story to tell. It was about a hardworking woman who had made her way in the world. And like Bayless, Springer saw her story as *her* story, not an emblem for the oppressed sisterhood of America. I knew I was in trouble as soon as I asked Springer if she was proud of having broken the glass ceiling.

"I'm no feminist," Springer replied. "No way. Not me."

As I asked her one question after another about gender

politics, Springer gave me a look that Miss Kitty used to give Festus, indicating that, although she found me entertaining, she thought I was a fool. Springer was pro-choice and pro-gun, but she didn't see what being a woman had to do with either. She maintained that during the campaign of 1998, gender was never an issue. "It was almost like the voters woke up afterward and said, 'Look what we've done.' It was that way for the women who got elected, too. During the campaign we never gave our gender a thought."

Stymied, I searched for a question that would redeem the interview. Maybe Springer and the other women who ran Arizona hadn't set out to become role models, I thought. But they'd been in office over a year now. "Have you noticed anything," I said, desperately, "that women officeholders do differently from men?"

Springer replied, "Not a damn thing."

The president of the senate, Brenda Burns, had only a few moments to spare before returning to the chamber. Giving me the answer I had by now come to expect, Burns, an elegant, dark-haired woman in her late forties, told me that women had risen to the top of the Republican Party in Arizona because of their abilities, not their gender. "Every one of us would tell you that," she said. Was there anything Republicans should do to reach out to women? Aside from making sure that no one was discriminated against, no. People needed to be judged on their merits, and the GOP was good at doing just that. "If you look at the presidential nominees currently, it is the Republican Party that has both a woman [Elizabeth Dole] and a black man [Alan Keyes] up as candidates. That really is one of the core beliefs of the Republican Party—that it looks at people on their merits."

When I asked if women conducted themselves in office any differently from men, Burns chuckled. Since so many women raised families—she has three children herself—they got used to juggling a lot of different tasks at once. "That does come in handy," Burns said. Then she had to run.

Governor Jane Dee Hull was polite, but the briskness with which she answered my questions made it clear that she had more important matters to attend to than gender politics. In her mid-sixties, the grandmother of eight, Hull has auburn hair, a birdlike nose, and bright, piercing eyes. While all the women with whom I spoke made me feel silly, Governor Hull made me feel ignorant, too. Women had always played a prominent role in the state, she said. When Arizona held its constitutional convention in 1910—two years before Arizona became a state and ten years before the Nineteenth Amendment gave women the vote—a dozen women participated. "Women came out here in covered wagons," Hull said. "They gave birth along the side of the trail with Indians attacking them." Compared with giving birth while dodging arrows, drafting a constitution must have been a piece of cake.

How had women risen to positions of such prominence in the Arizona GOP? It was a simple matter of seniority, the governor said. A cadre of capable women had become active in the party, then risen just the way men would have risen. Did the governor consider herself a feminist? No. Did women conduct themselves any differently in office from men? Only in small ways. "Governor Fife Symington preceded me," Governor Hull said. "Fife is by nature more confrontational." That was putting it mildly. Like his fellow Republican, Governor Mecham, before him, Governor Symington, forced to vacate his office in the midst of a scandal, had launched vicious attacks on his political enemies. (While Mecham, accused of misusing state funds, was ultimately acquitted, Symington was convicted of bank fraud.) "I think women are much more willing to bring people to the table and sit down and talk about an issue." Women, in other words, behaved like adults.

Journal entry:

This afternoon, as the plane back to California gained altitude, I found myself looking down on the shimmering skyscrapers and tidy green lawns of Phoenix, a city thrusting out into the desert at the rate of an acre an hour. Real estate, tourism, banking, insurance, technology—below lay all the infinite variety of human activity in a free society. Imagine it, I thought. All of that being overseen by a few tough Republican ladies.

CALLING KELLYANNE

On the one hand I had Jack, who ascribed the gender gap to the credulity and passivity of women. On the other I had the women officeholders of Arizona, who were so obviously noncredulous and nonpassive that I hadn't even dared to raise Jack's point of view in their presence. Confused, I turned to Kellyanne Fitzpatrick. Kellyanne, thirty-three, is the president of her own firm, the Polling Company, based in Washington, D.C. I hoped that, since she is both a professional political consultant, like Jack, and an immensely successful Republican woman, like the officeholders with whom I spoke in Arizona, Kellyanne could clear things up. She began by disabusing me of the notion that two of the so-called women's issues, guns and abortion, had anything to do with the gender gap.

It was true that women disliked guns, Kellyanne explained. "To many women, guns represent the last tiny basket of things in this world that they simply can't control. Women are better educated than they used to be. They're self-sufficient economically. But they still can't control kids opening fire in classrooms for no reason." Yet their dislike of guns doesn't mean women dislike the GOP. On the contrary, their dislike of guns draws them to the GOP at least as much as it repels them from it. Why? The Republican Party is tough on crime.

"If Republicans anchor themselves to 'do nothing' about guns when women are crying out, 'do something,' that will cost them," Kellyanne said. "But that's not what Republicans are doing." Although they defend the right to bear arms more vigorously than Democrats, Republicans nevertheless support the registration of handguns, bans on assault weapons, and so on. You might conclude that the GOP's stand on guns is inconsistent. You cannot conclude that it accounts for the gender gap.

Nor can you attribute the gender gap to the GOP's pro-life stand. "Abortion is an issue that has lost intensity and will continue to do so," Kellyanne said. "It's a case of 'the fetus beat us.'" A minor medical development, the widespread use of sonograms, has made a large political difference. "People will find a sonogram on the bulletin board of a colleague while she's expecting, or their father will fax them a sonogram with a note that says, 'Here's your newest cousin!' It's nonconfrontational. Nobody sticks the sonogram in their face and says, 'This is a baby, damn it!' or 'This is nothing but a pollywog, damn it!' People just see the sonogram, and they get used to the idea that the fetus is already part of somebody's family." Abortion remains an issue, of course. But science is quickly replacing religion as the framework in which the debate over abortion takes place. Women therefore see pro-life Republicans less as strident moralists, attempting to impose their views on others, than as advocates, discussing medical facts. Women still feel more strongly about abortion than do men. Yet they do so in numbers much too small to account for the gender gap. For that matter, those who feel most strongly about abortion tend to vote for Republicans, not against them.

After making certain I understood that guns and abortion, the two issues you're most likely to hear cited as the reasons for the gender gap, actually have nothing to do with the gender gap, Kellyanne let me in on the true reasons. "There are three," she said, "and number one is a big one. Men and women just fundamentally differ about the role of government in their lives."

Men want government out of their lives, and their approach toward dealing with it can be neatly summarized using vivid verbs. Cut. Slash. Hack. Hew. Bash. "Women have their feet pointed in the same direction, but their pace of change is a lot less rapid and aggressive," Kellyanne explained. The female approach to dealing with government can best be summarized using tepid verbs. Trim. Modify. Adjust. "Republicans keep saying they want a revolution. But every time they do that, they lose women's votes. Women don't want a Republican revolution. They want a Republican—what would the word be? Something smaller. They want a Republican ripple."

The second reason for the gender gap was a matter of the heart—specifically, that women are uncertain Republicans actually have hearts. "I call it the compassion gap," Kellyanne said. Women see Democrats as decent, warm, caring human beings, the sort of people with whom they'd be willing to leave their children for a weekend, while they see Republicans as ogres of the sort who might eat their children for lunch. Democrats nice, Republicans nasty. Women just can't get the comparison out of their minds. "Whoever gets the GOP presidential nomination, all that Al Gore or Bill Bradley will have to do is run ads wrapping Republicans who come across as nasty—people like Jesse Helms and Tom DeLay— around his neck. With women, it's an obvious strategy."

The final reason for the gender gap was the media. "Men and women receive their news and information from essentially different outlets," Kellyanne explained. While men are 12 percent more likely than women to read a newspaper every day, women are 14 percent more likely than men to cite ABC, NBC, CBS, or CNN as their primary source of news. "Women actually assign a certain level of guilt to holding a newspaper in their hands, because when they're reading a newspaper, that is literally all they can do at that moment." With the television droning in the background, by contrast, women can fold laundry, make dinner, or review their children's homework.

When women do have a moment to spare, they curl up with a woman's magazine. Add up the circulation of just six magazines—*Better Homes and Gardens, Family Circle, Good Housekeeping, Ladies' Home Journal, Woman's Day,* and *McCall's*—and you'd find that they reached more than 30 million women. "These magazines get women to trust them by giving their readers health and nutrition information—articles like 'Avoiding Risky Vitamins for Your Kids' or 'Caring for an Elderly Parent,'" Kellyanne said. "But the editorial content is all to the left. And when the magazines put Mrs.

Clinton on the cover, readers think Hillary must be as wholesome as good nutrition."

Women differ from Republicans on the role of government, find Republicans wanting in compassion, and receive their information from news organizations that are, broadly speaking, liberal, not conservative, in their makeup. "When it comes to the gender gap," Kellyanne said, "those three reasons are it."

Kellyanne's analysis was based on years of experience in conducting polls and interpreting their results. But it still left me feeling a little uneasy. Although she and Jack had only one explicit point of agreement—that women get their news from different sources than do men—her view and Jack's came to pretty much the same thing. Women were . . . irrational. If men said they wanted to slash, bash, and hew the government, they were expressing a reasoned assessment of their own interests. Less government would mean lower taxes, and therefore bigger paychecks. But if women said they wanted only to trim or adjust government, what did they mean? That the federal government, which each year spends more than $1.8 *trillion*, an amount equal to a fifth of the total goods and services produced by the entire economy, is indeed too big, but only by a smidgen? What sense did that make? And if women found Republicans lacking in compassion, what was their basis for doing so? Reading *Cosmopolitan* every month but never picking up a newspaper? The economic boom that Ronald Reagan began has done a lot more good for the poor than any welfare program ever did. Even such supposedly heartless Republicans as Senator Jesse Helms and Representative Tom DeLay have done a lot of good for the poor, preventing the Clinton administration from enacting tax hikes and spending programs that would have impeded the boom. Can't women see that?

Of course there are exceptional women, like those running Arizona. But the reason for the gender gap is that millions of women can't *think*. I didn't like that conclusion. But I couldn't see any way around it.

POOF! THE GAP VANISHES

Then I spoke to Newt Gingrich again.

It was a chance meeting, as if in a novel. This was fitting. My exploration of gender politics had started to seem like a flawed work of nineteenth-century fiction, traveling in circles instead of proceeding to a destination. Appearing from nowhere—actually, he was visiting California for a couple of days from Washington—Gingrich provided the sudden denouement that permitted me to draw the effort to a close.

"If you want to make the gender gap disappear, all you have to do is make just one statistical correction," Gingrich explained.

The correction involved single women. Once single women are removed from the data pool, Republicans get about as many votes among women—limited, now, to married women—as they do among men. What accounts for the statistical anomaly? What leads married women to vote Republican while single women vote Democratic? Economics.

By and large, married women are economically secure. They feel no need for the government to help or protect them, so they are content to vote for the GOP, the party of limited government. But single women are often economically exposed. Young single women, particularly those with children, frequently depend on welfare, food stamps, and other forms of government assistance. Old single women, many of them widows—and since women tend to outlive men, there are millions more widows than widowers—frequently depend on Social Security and Medicare. Young and old, single women vote for the Democratic Party, which they correctly see as the party of the welfare state.

"It's simple. The gender gap is a function of women who rely on government as opposed to those who don't," Gingrich explained.

No doubt all that Kellyanne Fitzpatrick had told me was true. No doubt even a great deal of what Jack had said possessed a basis in fact. But the gender gap doesn't exist because women are irrational. It exists because they are rational. Just as any economist or political scientist would predict, women vote their self-interest.

Journal entry:
The Nineteenth Amendment wasn't a mistake after all. I can't wait to tell Edita.

YOU GOTTA HAVE HEART

Before running into Gingrich, I had concluded that all the GOP could do about the gender gap was learn to live with it—that and take out ads in *Redbook* and *Vogue*. Now I thought I saw at least a couple of steps Republicans might take. The first would be to start treating single mothers with respect.

Society has played a rotten trick on these women, telling them that easy divorce, contraceptives, and abortion on demand would liberate them. They haven't. They have liberated men, permitting them to skip out on the children they father— after all, when a single woman has a child these days, the father can tell himself that she should have used the pill or had an abortion. If every American followed the precepts of traditional morality, there would certainly be far fewer single mothers. But to the almost ten million women who are already single mothers, Republican talk about traditional morality can sound like mere sanctimony. Picture it. You're a single mother, trying to cook all the meals, change all the diapers, and wipe all the noses by yourself. Then one day while you're doing the laundry, a Republican appears on television to drone on about traditional morality. What do you do? It's obvious. Pitch the flatiron at him.

Tommy Thompson, the Republican governor of Wisconsin, has demonstrated one way to replace sanctimony toward single mothers with tangible help. Thompson has reformed Wisconsin's welfare system, cutting the state's welfare rolls by more than half. Yet even as he has moved single mothers off welfare, Thompson has provided them with special assistances. One Thompson reform helps to ensure that deadbeat dads make their child support payments. Another makes certain that as single mothers undergo training and then enter the job market, they receive help in locating and paying for child care. Yet another ensures that teenage mothers receive child care and transportation for free. Wisconsin now spends more on single mothers and their children than it did before Thompson put his reforms into effect. The reforms aren't perfect. Some children would no doubt be better off if their mothers stayed home. Still and all, Thompson's reforms represent a serious effort to promote self-reliance among single mothers while treating them with respect. Republicans elsewhere could do a lot worse.

After according respect to single mothers, the second step for the GOP would be obvious. Accord the same respect to single old ladies.

Forty-five percent of women sixty-five or older are widowed. More than two thirds of them live alone, many cut off even from their own families. My brother and I saw this with our own mother just a couple of years ago. We always thought of ourselves as close to her. When my brother moved from the East Coast to Seattle, and then, some years later, I followed him west, moving to California, it never occurred to either of us that we were leaving her behind. Then she fell ill. There she was, a widow in a retirement complex in North Carolina, all the way on the other side of the country, suddenly unable to care for herself. When we were able to move her to Seattle, where she would be close to my brother and his family, she told us that her friends in the retirement complex envied her. "You'd be surprised how many people here never see their children or grandchildren," she said. Exactly.

Now, the problem of caring for the elderly is complicated—and the GOP scarcely needs a writer like me mouthing off about new programs. I wouldn't even know how to estimate the costs. (All I can tell you is that the program I kept imagining while my mother was sick—free around-the-clock care by nurses with the compassion of nuns and the expertise of MDs—wouldn't be cheap.) But it has crossed my mind that the GOP might propose a few faith-based initiatives, programs that would shift resources for the elderly from federal bureaucracies to private organizations, including religious groups. Of course no Republican wants to see church groups taken over by the feds. But since the church workers who called on my mother were always a lot more cheerful and friendly than the county social workers the hospital sent, I can't help thinking that religious groups might be able to provide old people with better care than can the government. In other words, faith-based initiatives might work.

The Republican Party's principal appeal to women, I suspect, will always remain just what the women in Arizona found in the GOP: a willingness to judge women and men alike according to their individual merits. If the women in Arizona had been Democrats, they would have had to take me seriously when I asked them about gender politics, producing paragraphs of feminist oratory. As Republicans, they were free to dismiss me as a fool. That was no mean liberation in itself.

Can the Republican Party ever close the gender gap? The outlook isn't encouraging. What the GOP preaches is self-reliance. What single mothers and widows want is help. This is a standoff from which the Democratic Party is only too happy to profit, promising to shower single women with government largesse. All the same, the GOP ought to do its best to appeal to single women, making its case for self-reliance while providing whatever assistance it can. It might at least narrow the gender gap. Then again, it might not. But showing a little heart would do the party good.

Chapter Eight

ON THE BORDER OF THE FINKELSTEIN BOX

Journal entry:

*A retired schoolteacher: "Is this your first time in Fresno?
It is? Well, you'll find that people here are nothing like
people in San Francisco or L.A. We're more like people in
Iowa. We pride ourselves on it."*

*A Mexican baby-sitter: "Oh, if I could become legal, I
would. But they won't let me. And I can't afford to pay the
taxes anyway. My daughter and her children all live on the
money I make in this country."*

Arthur Finkelstein, a Republican political consultant,
uses a simple device to show his clients the way the
country divides politically. As you can see, Finkelstein
draws a lopsided box on a map of the United States.
Inside the box, Republicans do well, while Democrats do
badly. Outside it, Democrats do well, while Republicans do
badly. In states whose largest centers of population lie inside
the box, for example, no Democratic candidate for the Senate won a majority in the election of 1996 except Mary Landrieu of Louisiana, and her majority was so narrow—just a
few thousand votes—that her Republican opponent, charging

fraud, was able to persuade the Senate to conduct an investigation. (The Senate found a number of irregularities in the vote count, but sustained Landrieu in her seat.) In the same states two years later, in the election of 1998, five Democratic candidates for the Senate won majorities, but three of the five did so by less than 10 percent, while one of the five, Harry Reid of Nevada, did so by a bare one tenth of 1 percent. In states whose largest centers of population lie outside the box, by contrast, no Republican candidate for the Senate won a majority in the election of 1996, while two years later, in the election of just three Republican candidates for the Senate won such majorities, one of them, Peter Fitzgerald of Illinois, managing to do so by a mere 2.9 percent. Inside the box, Republican governors are entirely pro-life. Outside the box, Republican governors are often pro-choice.

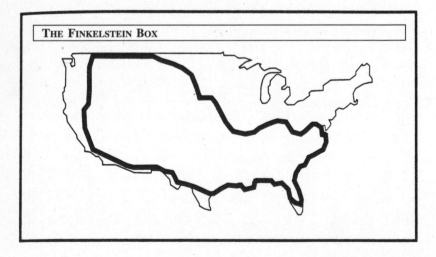

THE FINKELSTEIN BOX

A simple, lopsided box—yet it cleaves the country cleanly in two.

When I first learned about the Finkelstein Box, it brought

to mind a valley in Switzerland where I skied when I was a bachelor. I stayed in a village called Rougemont. Three miles up the road was a village called Saanen. Everyone in Rougemont was a French-speaking Catholic. Everyone in Saanen was a German-speaking Protestant. Each day I'd wake up in Rougement, exchange a few words of French with the waitress over breakfast, spend half a day skiing, then have lunch in Saanen, where I'd sit in silence, unable to exchange a few words with the waitress because I spoke no German. How remarkable, I'd think, that these people have preserved their separate identities. How quaint. How European.

But a cultural border here? In the United States? This country is supposed to be a melting pot. Immigrants are supposed to arrive from other countries, learn English, begin intermarrying with those already here, and become, well, *American.* The distinction between the two political identities, one Republican, the other Democratic, that the Finkelstein Box delineates may not be as sharp as the distinction between the two cultural identities that I encountered in Switzerland. But it's still a lot sharper than any distinction I'd ever thought existed in the United States.

Studying the Finkelstein Box, I noticed that it carved its way through the middle of California. Like the rest of the California coast, the San Francisco peninsula, which includes Silicon Valley, where I live, lay outside the box. Most of the towns of the central valley lay inside it. Why? What could be so different about the coast and the central valley? I decided to choose one town inside the box, then pay it a visit. My finger fell on Fresno.

TO FAR FRESNO

Journal entry:

As I drove south down the San Francisco peninsula, I listened, as is my habit, to the warm, comforting tones of Bob Edwards on National Public Radio's Morning Edition. *Then, going up through the Pacheco Pass over the Diablo Mountains, I lost the signal. When I came down into the central valley and hit the scan button, the radio made its way through half a dozen country music stations before it found a grainy NPR signal. Bob Edwards's voice came and went, trading places with static. Finally I gave up, listening to Garth Brooks instead.*

Country music. How did Finkelstein know?

Making the three-hour drive to Fresno, I kept a running list of first impressions, noting the ways the central valley differed from the San Francisco peninsula, as if I were a tourist, which, come to think of it, I was. First I noticed the difference in radio stations that I commented on in my journal. Then I noticed the difference in cars. On the peninsula, the preferred vehicles are BMWs, Mercedes-Benzes, Jaguars, and other prestigious foreign makes—even the odd Rolls-Royce shows up from time to time, wallowing down University Avenue in Palo Alto or nosing into a parking place at the Stanford Shopping Center. But after the turnoff for Route Five, the interstate to Los Angeles, foreign cars in the central valley all but disappeared, replaced by endless Fords, Chevrolets, Dodges, Buicks, and Oldsmobiles. The few luxury cars that I spotted were almost without exception big Cadillacs or fat Lincoln Town Cars, the kinds of cars that retired farmers buy, as if to compensate their bodies after years spent in the seats of tractors. For several miles I found myself stuck behind a pickup truck. Something about the truck seemed unusual. When a straw broke free from one of the bales of hay the truck was hauling, smacking against my windshield, I realized what it was. The truck in front of me was the first pickup I'd seen in months that was being used for a purpose other than show.

The most striking difference between the San Francisco peninsula and the central valley proved so all-encompassing that it took a while to sink in. Back in Silicon Valley, people made money. At least that's the way I always thought of it. I knew, of course, that what they really made was computer equipment and, increasingly, software. But since so many people in Silicon Valley labored all day without ever making anything you could hold in your hands—true, you could hold a floppy disk containing the software in your hands, but all you were holding was the disk, not the software, not *it*—they might as well have been alchemists, transforming thoughts in their minds directly into money in their bank accounts. In the central valley, people didn't make money. They grew food. For mile upon mile, I found myself passing orchards, vineyards, and fields of rice, cotton, and alfalfa. Granted, the agriculture that takes place in the central valley is among the most sophisticated on earth—Fresno County itself produces more than $3 billion a year in agricultural goods, more, as far as I can discover, than any other county in the nation. But driving through the central valley still felt appealingly simple and basic. All you had to do to see how people made their living was look out the window. I might as well have been touring Kansas. Before long I noticed a bumper sticker on a Lincoln Town Car that almost persuaded me I was. "Live Better," the bumper sticker said. "Vote Republican."

In Silicon Valley, of course, most voters would have found the bumper sticker ridiculous. Up and down Silicon Valley, from San Jose in the south to Burlingame in the north, city councilmen and women are predominantly Democratic. Silicon Valley is represented in the state assembly by five Democrats and just one Republican and in the state senate by three Democrats. Of the four members of Congress who represent Silicon Valley, three, Tom Lantos, Anna Eshoo, and Zoe Lofgren, are Democrats, while the fourth, Tom Campbell, is by any reckoning one of the three or four most liberal Republicans in the House. But in Fresno, following the advice on the bumper sticker and voting Republican amounts to a way of life. Although Fresno is represented in the state senate by a Democrat—it lies on the edge of a huge senate district, drawn to include large numbers of Democrats—it is represented in the state assembly by a Republican. The member of Congress who represents most of Fresno, George Radonovich, is a Republican so conservative that he supported the 1995 government shutdown even though it closed Yosemite National Park, a large portion of which lies in his district, and so popular that in 1998 he ran for reelection unopposed. The mayor of Fresno, Jim Patterson, is a Republican so conservative that before entering politics he made his living as a radio evangelist. By the time I reached the outskirts of Fresno I had counted another half dozen pro-Republican bumper stickers—in six years on the San Francisco peninsula, the only bumper sticker I could recall using the word "Republican" said "Friends Don't Let Friends Vote Republican"—then, near the city limits, I came upon an enormous billboard proclaiming, "Democrats Promote Immoral Living." When I tell you the billboard would have been unimaginable in Silicon Valley, I mean that literally. I spent the next several minutes trying to imagine it. I couldn't.

When I reached the city I missed my exit, inadvertently giving myself two chances to look over downtown Fresno, once driving south before I figured out my mistake, once backtracking north. From both directions downtown looked almost empty. Rising from the bare streets rose several blocks of modest brick and stone structures that probably dated from the early years of the twentieth century, a couple of boxlike office towers (lawyers and accountants have to have their offices somewhere), and a single modern building, pyramidal, glass-clad, and gleaming in the sun, that I later learned was Fresno's city hall and one attempt at urban renewal. After backtracking, I got off the interstate onto Shaw Avenue. Shaw Avenue looked as full of traffic as downtown had looked empty. For miles, it took me past shopping malls, schools, fast-food restaurants, and video stores. The scene was one of prosperous suburbia. I turned left onto Fresno Street. At the intersection of Fresno and Barstow, I reached my destination, Hope Lutheran Church.

Pastor Donald Bentz, the father of a Stanford grad who once worked for me, introduced me to the three members of his congregation, each a Republican, that he had asked to join us for coffee in the church hall. One was a dentist. Another was a small businessman. The third was a retired schoolteacher, now serving, according to the card that she handed across the table, as the "Program Coordinator for the Republican Central Committee of Fresno County." We spent a couple of hours talking about politics. All three wanted lower taxes and a stronger national defense. All three were disgusted with President Clinton. One considered Steve Forbes the best Republican candidate for president; two preferred George W. Bush. While we talked, I kept having a strange sensation. I seemed to recognize these people. I knew their opinions. I even felt comfortable with the cadences of their speech. Then it struck me. I had grown up with them.

Not with these very people, of course. But with people so much like them—white, Protestant, decent, hardworking— that I might just as easily have been sharing a cup of coffee with the dentist, the small businessman, and the retired school-teacher in the hall of First Congregational Church in Bing-hamton, New York, as in the hall of Hope Lutheran Church in Fresno, California. Once I thought of them, the parallels between Fresno and my hometown seemed so obvious that I was surprised they hadn't occurred to me sooner.

Both Fresno and my hometown were Republican, of course. But that seemed almost the least of it. Like Fresno, the group of communities in which I grew up, the Triple Cities, were modest in size. (The population of Fresno is about 360,000. The population of the Triple Cities—a clus-ter of towns made up of Binghamton, Johnson City, Endicott, and a couple of suburbs, including Vestal, where we lived— was, when I was growing up, about 250,000.) The Triple Cities may have been a manufacturing rather than an agri-cultural center, but they felt the same as Fresno in at least two regards. One was that the Triple Cities were close to the land. From downtown Binghamton you could drive fifteen minutes in any direction, pull over, roll down your window, and hear a dairy cow moo. The other was that people in the Triple Cities earned their living by making objects you could see and touch. When I was little, the principal employer was the Endicott-Johnson Shoe Company. During the summers, when workers opened the windows, you could watch men stripped to the waist hauling stacks of hides around the factory floor. By the time I was a teenager, the dominant concern was IBM. I know that name may bring to mind images of high technology. But in those days IBM was manufacturing the first mainframes—big, bulky machines with moving parts—and the plants in which it did so bore a lot more resemblance to the old E.-J. shoe factories than to the pristine corporate campuses of Silicon Valley.

The parallels between the Triple Cities and Fresno extended into the details. People in the Triple Cities, like people in Fresno, drove American cars and listened to country music—I can still remember my piano teacher's irritation when the classical radio station in town switched to an all-country format. Downtown Binghamton even looked like downtown Fresno. It comprised a few blocks of brick and stone structures that dated from the early years of the twentieth century, a couple of modest office towers, and a modern government complex that represented the city's principal attempt at urban renewal after a mall opened on the edge of town, drawing all the retail business out of town with it.

Here I was in Fresno, California, a city in which I had never set foot, and I felt, if not exactly at home—I had gotten lost coming in, after all—then certainly more comfortable and at ease than I had ever felt on the San Francisco peninsula, where I had lived for six years. Now, I like the San Francisco peninsula. Silicon Valley is endlessly fascinating. But whereas I enjoy the people I meet there, the people I was meeting in Fresno were people I *knew*. How could this have happened?

"It's not just party membership that the box tracks," Arthur

Finkelstein told me over the telephone the day after I visited Fresno. "It's psychographics."

"Psychographics" is a term of art used in the disciplines, if they may be called that, of advertising and marketing. It describes the interrelated attitudes, values, lifestyles, opinions, demographics, and so on that lead people to buy one product instead of another. If you are a large food corporation, for example, you might develop psychographic research showing that people who live in cities, listen to classical music, and watch soap operas tend to purchase whole wheat bread instead of white. Arthur Finkelstein has applied psychographics to politics. Inside the Finkelstein Box, he has discovered, lie people with a certain set of characteristics. They tend to live in regions dominated by towns and medium-sized cities rather than by large urban centers. They are for the most part white and Protestant. They tend to go to church regularly, to drive American cars, to listen to country music—and to vote Republican. I may think pronounced regional cultures better suited to Europe than to the United States, but there is a pronounced regional culture inside the Finkelstein Box all the same. I reflected that culture myself. These days the Triple Cities lie outside the Finkelstein Box. But when I was growing up there a quarter of a century ago, Arthur Finkelstein assured me, my hometown lay inside the box. Hence the reason Fresno seemed so familiar. In driving there, I had returned to the country I knew in my youth: the heartland.

"But why?" I asked Finkelstein. "Why should listening to country music, driving American cars, and living in medium-sized towns all go with voting Republican?" Finkelstein gave me the reply of an honest man. "I don't know," he said. "They just do."

They just do.

Here we find ourselves once more confronting the lesson that David Brady took such glee in teaching me. When he and I talked over the history of the Republican Party, you will recall, David insisted that people belong to political parties for all sorts of reasons, a lot of which don't have anything to do with politics. Often, David argued, people inherit their party affiliation right along with their ancestry and religion. Arthur Finkelstein makes an argument that is related but distinct enough to stand on its own. Party affiliation, Finkelstein claims, represents one more element in the constellation of characteristics with which a person expresses his culture. People in Rougemont, Switzerland, speak French, attend Catholic churches, and eat Gruyère cheese. People in the Finkelstein Box drive Fords and Chevrolets, listen to Garth Brooks, and vote Republican.

As the party on the inside of the Finkelstein Box, the GOP is the party of the great American interior. As far as it goes, that sounds reassuring. Every party needs a political base. The heartland would seem a good one. Yet there is a problem here. Cultures are durable. While living just walking distance apart, the people of Rougemont and Saanen, Switzerland, have maintained their separate identities for centuries. Thus if the GOP represents the culture of the heartland, then those who belong to a different culture—those, that is, whose psychographics place them outside the Finkelstein Box—will persistently elude it.

To some extent the Republican Party has already learned to live with this situation. The GOP makes do without the support of the media—you will notice that the major media centers, New York, Washington, D.C., and Los Angeles, all lie outside the box. And Republicans have learned to win at least occasional support from white Catholics, heavy concentrations of whom lie outside the box, in the Northeast and upper Midwest.

Yet one group outside the box has the GOP alarmed.

"I noticed that there are odd slivers of certain states lying outside the box," I said when I spoke to Arthur Finkelstein. "What's going on with the southern tip of Florida and the southern edges of Arizona, New Mexico, and Texas?"

"Hispanics," Finkelstein replied. "Those are all places where there are lots of Hispanics, and Hispanics are definitely outside the box."

THE BOX WITHIN THE BOX

Journal entry:

Over breakfast last month I asked John Morgan how he would sum up the difference between the Republican and Democratic parties.

"The GOP," John replied, "represents the descendants of people who came here in colonial and early American times. They're the ones who took the land and settled it. The Democrats represent the descendants of everybody else. It's sort of the first colonists versus the people who came through Ellis Island."

Today I had lunch with Ron Unz. Ron had been studying some statistics.

"Did you realize," Ron asked, "that here in California, white people are already *in the minority?"*

The difficulty that Hispanics pose for the Republican Party has all the inescapability of a mathematical proposition. It can be stated in just four points.

Point one: The Hispanic population is growing more quickly than the population as a whole—since 1990, Hispanics have increased their numbers by 38 percent, rising to 31 million, while other Americans have increased their numbers by just 9 percent. By 2005, Hispanics will make up 14 percent of the population, passing African-Americans, who make up 13 percent, as the nation's largest minority. Then, by the middle of the twenty-first century, a date that my children will see even if I do not, Hispanics will account for a full one quarter of the population.

Point two: Hispanics vote Democratic. For the last two decades, Hispanics have consistently given Democrats between 65 and 75 percent of their vote. Some Hispanics, notably Cubans, vote Republican, but they make up only a small proportion of the Hispanic whole. Even when Hispanics live inside the Finkelstein Box—300,000 live in Fresno County— they occupy, so to speak, a box within the box, voting Democratic. It is Hispanics, for example, who ensure that Fresno is represented in the state senate by a Democrat.

Point three: During the 1980s the Republican Party achieved rough electoral parity with the Democratic Party for the first time in half a century. If the GOP cannot persuade a sizable proportion of Hispanics to become Republicans, then the GOP will revert to minority status and stay there.

Point four: Broadly speaking, as my friend John Morgan points out, the Republican Party represents the descendants of those who arrived in America during the colonial or federalist periods. Of all the immigrant groups who came afterward—the Irish, the Italians, the Jews, the Slavs—the GOP has failed to make even one—just one—a loyal part of the Republican constituency. This doesn't necessarily doom the GOP to fail with Hispanics. But it certainly isn't encouraging.

In California, where the trend toward a large Hispanic population is further advanced than elsewhere in the nation, Republicans have responded to Hispanics in two ways. Both bear examining. First a few words of background.

FROM WHITE TO BROWN

For decades a smaller proportion of the population of California was made up of minorities than was the case in almost any other large state. Few African-Americans lived in California until after the Second World War. Even then the proportion of African-Americans in the state never exceeded 7 percent, about half the national average of 13 percent. As late as 1970 nine out of ten Californians were white.

Then the inundation began.

Between 1970 and 1995, two million legal immigrants entered California, a quarter of the total that entered the entire nation. At least half the legal immigrants to California were Hispanic. During the same period hundreds of thousands of illegal immigrants entered the state. The number of illegal immigrants can only be estimated, but even the lowest estimates place it at one million. At least 80 percent were Hispanic. Not only were Hispanics arriving in large numbers, once they settled in California they gave birth in large numbers. The Hispanic birth rate proved so high that by 1991 the number of babies born to Hispanics exceeded the number born to whites, even though whites still outnumbered Hispanics by two to one.

The millions of Hispanic immigrants to California were joined by at least a million Asian immigrants and by hundreds of thousands of immigrants from the Near East. Together, they represented an influx so great that Ron Unz, who has made a close study of immigrants in California, believes they turned the white population of the state into a minority sometime during the 1980s. The peculiarities of federal racial classifications make it impossible to say this for certain. The government used to force everyone into one of four categories: white, Asian, black, and Hispanic. Hence in government statistics the hundreds of thousands of Iranian and Egyptian immigrants to California actually served to make the state "whiter," offsetting the rising numbers of Asians and Hispanics. After attempting to correct for this anomaly, Ron has concluded that white people of the kind that the term "white" ordinarily implies—that is, European whites—found themselves outnumbered in California fifteen or more years ago.

FIRST GOODWILL, THEN ANIMOSITY

For a time the most noteworthy aspect of relations between white Californians and the new, mostly Hispanic immigrants was how well they got along. Even in areas where the concentration of immigrants was heaviest, relations proved peaceful. For example, between 1976 and 1996 the five counties that make up the Los Angeles basin—Los Angeles, Orange, Riverside, San Bernardino, and Ventura—saw immigrants inflate their population by 40 percent. About a million new immigrants arrived from Asia while more than two million arrived from Mexico and elsewhere in Latin America. In the Balkans, a population shift of half that magnitude would have prompted open warfare. In the Los Angeles basin, the economy and political system absorbed the new immigrants without fuss.

Then in the early 1990s the white attitude toward the new immigrants shifted.

Ron Unz notes several causes. A recession struck. Although it proved mild in most of the nation, the recession was severe in California, largely because the end of the Cold War led to heavy cutbacks in Southern California's aerospace industry. As tens of thousands of Californians were losing their jobs, the California real estate bubble burst, causing housing values to plummet. Then, after the verdict in the Rodney King trial, rioting erupted. "It's impossible to overstate the effect of the Rodney King rioting on white Californians," Ron says. Much of the violence pitted African-Americans against immigrants, especially Hispanics and Koreans, who had begun to displace African-Americans from their neighborhoods. When white Californians turned on their televisions, they saw smoke spreading across the sky.

For decades white Americans had moved to the Golden State because it seemed just that, golden—a land of sunshine, good jobs, affordable housing, and excellent schools. Now California was golden no longer. When its white inhabitants looked around, wondering who might be to blame, they saw a lot of faces, especially brown faces, that they weren't even sure belonged there.

JUST INSANE

As I've said, Republicans in California tried dealing with Hispanics in two different ways. The first was to ostracize them.

Written by a group of anti-immigrant activists in Orange County, Proposition 187 appeared on the California ballot in November 1994. As mentioned earlier, the initiative would have denied illegal immigrants an array of government services. Proposition 187 would have prevented illegal immigrants from receiving care at public hospitals and—the initiative's most inflammatory measure—it would have excluded their children from California's public schools. "Prop. 187 would have forced hundreds of thousands of children out of school," Ron Unz, who fought the measure, told me. Governor Pete Wilson, running in 1994, endorsed the initiative, swinging the full weight of the California Republican Party behind it.

"What do Hispanics value most?" Ron Unz said. "Their families. So what did Republicans do? They went after Hispanic children. It was just insane." In his late thirties, Ron grew up in Southern California. While studying at Stanford for a doctorate in engineering, he realized that he could write a software program that would prove useful to traders on Wall Street. In his spare time, he wrote the software, then founded a company called Wall Street Analytics. The company made him rich. Instead of retiring to play golf, Ron has devoted himself to politics. He is skinny, cerebral, and friendly. He speaks in measured tones, often pausing, even in midsentence, to think. A native of California, Ron is determined to reconcile the Republican Party with immigrants, especially Hispanic immigrants. Over lunch one afternoon, he argued that although Proposition 187 was intended to cut off services only to illegal immigrants, nobody should have been surprised when the measure offended legal immigrants. In many cases, legal and illegal immigrants belonged to the same families. For that matter, in many cases legal immigrants came here illegally themselves, acquiring legal status only in 1986, when President Reagan signed legislation granting amnesty to three million illegal immigrants. "Maybe Anglos think you can draw a line between legal and illegal immigrants, but try telling that to the Hispanics in this state," Ron said.

Proposition 187 passed overwhelmingly, receiving 59 percent of the vote. When it was blocked by the federal courts—the 1982 Supreme Court decision, *Plyler v. Doe*, requires states to provide public education for all children—Governor Wilson, who had been reelected, launched a legal fight on behalf of the measure that he pursued throughout his second term, associating the Republican Party with Proposition 187 for another four years. (In 1999, as we have seen, the measure was set aside as the result of arbitration.)

Proposition 187 may never have taken force, but its effects were felt all the same. Throughout the 1980s and the early 1990s, Hispanics in California cast between 30 and 40 percent of their votes for Republicans. In 1994, the year Proposition 187 was on the ballot, that figure fell to less than 20 percent. It has yet to recover. "Prop. 187 was a *catastrophe* for Republicans," Ron said. "It will take at least a couple of generations for Hispanics to forgive us."

Now, it is worth pausing to note that you didn't have to be rabidly anti-immigrant to support Proposition 187. After having lunch with Ron Unz, I had breakfast with former Governor Pete Wilson.

A former marine, Pete is still lean at 67. For a man who spent so much of his life in high office, he is utterly unassuming—when we walked into Il Fornaio, a high-tech gathering place in Palo Alto, the maître d' failed to recognize Pete, giving us a table against the back wall, perhaps the worst table in the dining room. Pete never complained. (As one diner after another approached the former governor to pay his respects, the maître d' looked perplexed, as if he was trying to figure out just how much of a mistake he had made.)

"Prop. 187 wasn't an anti-immigrant measure," Pete said. "It was the biggest taxpayer revolt since the Boston Tea Party." For years the federal government had failed to police the border with Mexico, permitting immigrants to stream into California illegally. Then the federal government had forced California to provide the illegal immigrants with billions of dollars' worth of services a year. "Those bastards in Washington were falling down on the job," Pete said, "and they were sticking our taxpayers with the bill." Pete spoke earnestly. His sincerity was transparent. He never had any intention of seeing children thrown out of school. He knew the initiative would get tied up in the courts instead. "That was part of the beauty of it," he said. Pete, who was convinced that *Plyler v. Doe* had been incorrectly decided, intended to take Proposition 187 all the way to the Supreme Court, forcing the Court to rule that the federal government, not the states, must bear the costs of caring for illegal immigrants.

A taxpayer revolt. Pete Wilson's stand sounds so reasonable, so Republican. Indeed, we have heard from one young man, Justin Adams, who joined the GOP largely because he admired the courage Wilson displayed in supporting Proposition 187. Justin on the one hand, several million Hispanics on the other. The problem is that this is not a winning calculation.

NATURAL REPUBLICANS

In 1996, two years after the passage of Proposition 187, Proposition 227 appeared on the California ballot. Written by Ron Unz himself, Proposition 227 was intended to ban bilingual education in the state's public schools. Ron's own mother had been born into a Yiddish-speaking household in Los Angeles, yet when she attended school she had learned English quickly. Bearing in mind his mother's experience, Ron based his initiative—the Unz Initiative, as it became known—on the proposition that Hispanics and other recent immigrants were no different from the generations of immigrants who had come to this country before them. Their children should not be taught in the native language of their parents. They should be taught in English.

The Unz Initiative represented the second approach to Hispanics that Republicans in California have attempted: treating Hispanics like everybody else.

In lining up support for the initiative, Ron recruited Alice Callaghan, a prominent left-wing activist, and several prominent Hispanics, including Jaime Escalante, the public school teacher portrayed in the movie *Stand and Deliver*. Ron made no effort to gather endorsements from prominent Republicans. "I was trying to win the support of Hispanics, not drive them away," Ron explained. "The last thing I wanted was an endorsement from Pete Wilson." Although many Republicans, including Pete Wilson, supported the measure—"Unz and I have our differences," Pete told me, "but he did a great thing with Prop. 227"—they did so quietly.

Ron's strategy almost worked.

Up until the week of the election, polls showed that more

than 60 percent of Hispanics supported the Unz Initiative.
Then opponents of the initiative began blanketing the state
with television ads, outspending Ron and the other backers
of the initiative by about twenty-five to one. (It later emerged
that money for the advertising campaign came largely from
the owner of Univision, the Spanish-language television net-
work. He seems to have opposed the Unz Initiative not because he thought it would fail but because he thought it
would work, reasoning that if Hispanic children learned English, he would lose his captive audience.) Although on election day itself the Unz Initiative passed with 61 percent of
the vote, just 40 percent of Hispanics voted for it. Ron was
downhearted—for a couple of weeks. Then polls began to
indicate that Hispanic support for the measure was re-
bounding. Soon Hispanics once again backed the Unz Initiative just as strongly as they had before the ad campaign
against it. "Political ads can only rent support," Ron says,
"not buy it.

"Hispanics didn't come here to go on welfare or rip off
California's taxpayers," Ron told me, "and their support for
Prop. 227 proves it. They came here to become Americans.
They have a strong work ethic. They believe in family values. As Catholics, they're pro-life. They're *natural* Republicans. But the Republican Party just can't seem to stop insulting
them."

As I was leaving Hope Lutheran Church, I noticed a Hispanic man in the reception area. Pastor Bentz told me he was
the janitor. I asked him to join me in the church hall for a
cup of coffee.

His name was Gregorio Leal, but he asked me to call him
Greg. In his mid-fifties, his hair still jet black, Greg explained

that he had been born into an extended migrant family. "My great-grandfather was the man of the family. He was the one who heard where there was work and decided where we would go next." The family followed farmwork from Texas, where Greg was born, throughout the Southwest and California. They moved constantly. The work—picking and packing crops— was hard. Greg decided early that he wanted a different life. "I just didn't want to run around," he said. "I didn't want to follow the crops."

In 1965 Greg joined the army. He performed three tours of duty in Vietnam.

"Three?" I asked. "I thought nobody had to do more than one."

"The second and third times, I volunteered," Greg replied. "I can't say I liked it. But compared to picking crops, it was easy money."

When Greg returned from Vietnam, he attended Fresno City College, earning a two-year associate's degree. Then he went to work as a custodian with the Fresno Unified School district. He married, bought a house, and raised three children, sending all three to college. When he retired he discovered that sitting at home all day bored him, so he went to work as the janitor at Hope Lutheran Church.

Greg had made something of himself. He had lived the American dream. The son of migrant workers, he had served in the military, gone to college, and become a husband, a father, and a hardworking, home-owning member of the middle class. He is a person any member of the GOP would be proud to call a fellow Republican. How does he vote? "I go both ways, but mostly Democratic," Greg said. What did he think of Proposition 187? "Deep inside myself, I thought Governor Wilson was wrong. I thought it came from prejudice. It's hard to forget."

Inside the Finkelstein Box, Greg was living in his own box. If the GOP had ever made an effort to persuade him to leave it, Greg hadn't noticed.

Chapter Nine

GEORGE AND RUDY'S EXCELLENT ADVENTURE

Journal entry:

George W. Bush isn't the only person whose plans have been upset by John McCain.

I did much of the reporting for this chapter when it seemed unthinkable that anyone other than George W. Bush would win the Republican presidential nomination. As I compose these words, Bush has lost to McCain in New Hampshire, came back to beat McCain in South Carolina, but then has lost to McCain once again in Michigan and Arizona—and my editor wants the manuscript at the end of this week. I would almost have been happier if by now Bush had suffered a clean defeat, finding himself forced to withdraw from the primary. At least then I could have tossed the Bush material out, rewriting the chapter as if I had known McCain would win all along.

Oh, well. I never said this would be a book of prognostication, just a travelogue. All I can do is describe the terrain as it appeared when I saw it. If Bush wins, I'll look prescient. If he loses, I'll look foolish. On the other hand, after devoting an entire book to the Republican Party, looking foolish should probably be the least of my worries.

Journal entry, composed three months after the journal entry above:

I simply cannot believe it. After I sent in the manuscript to be proofread, George W. Bush came back to defeat John McCain for the GOP presidential nomination, permitting me to feel certain that I would look prescient, not foolish, after all. But now Rudolph Giuliani, who I assumed would be the Republican senatorial candidate in New York, has announced that he has prostate cancer, that he has been conducting an extramarital affair, that he has decided to seek a formal separation from his wife, and that in view of his health and personal problems he is reconsidering his candidacy. "It's too late to change anything you've already written," my editor told me this afternoon, after Giuliani announced that he intends to separate from his wife. "But if you keep them short and get them to me tomorrow, you can add three paragraphs." Three paragraphs, of which this is the first.

What is there to say? Even now, Giuliani might decide to stay in the race. And if he dropped out, he could still choose to remain a force in Republican politics, perhaps running for governor of New York in 2002 if Pataki takes his place in this year's Senate race. I hope he does one or the other—and that by the end of Chapter Nine, the reader will see why. But if Giuliani decided to leave politics altogether, I couldn't blame him. How could I? Republicans believe in the primacy of private life. Attending to his health, straightening out his relationships with his wife and, as he described her, his "good friend," and devoting himself to

his two young children—that may be the most, well, the
most Republican course of action that Giuliani could take.

His decision is expected later this week. In the mean-
time, I'm trying to get used to the idea of looking foolish,
not prescient, all over again.

George W. Bush and Rudolph Giuliani. Two men could hardly differ more dramatically. In the notes I made during the day I spent traveling with George W. Bush in California in the spring of 1999, I described him as handsome, relaxed, a guy's guy, good at making small talk, the kind of man who would rather watch a football game than read a book and isn't embarrassed to say so, a person who wants to make everyone his friend. This last character-istic struck me most forcefully of all. At an event in Sacra-mento celebrating an athletic program for underprivileged teens, most of whom were black and Hispanic, Bush threw a football to one kid after another, tossing them passes in nice, tight spirals. That much was standard for a politician—posing for action shots with kids. But afterward, Bush lin-gered with the kids, talking to them. He shook their hands, patted them on the back, put his hand on their shoulders. They weren't even old enough to vote, but he wanted them to like him.

After spending time with Rudolph Giuliani at city hall a few months later, I described him in almost the opposite terms. Giuliani is striking rather than handsome, intense, cerebral, better at discussing policy than at making small talk, a man who conveys the impression that he actually reads memo-randa and briefing books of the kind with which his desk was littered, a person less interested in making people like him than any other politician I have ever met.

"Mr. Mayor, you've turned this city around," I said. "Why don't people like you more?"

Giuliani smiled and shrugged. "I just don't know," he replied. His tone indicated that he didn't particularly care, either.

One the product of a patrician WASP family, the other an Italian Catholic from Brooklyn. One the governor of Texas, a state in which people think of New York City as the very embodiment of everything that's wrong with America, the other the mayor of New York City, a metropolis in which Texas is the punch line of a joke. Yet there they are, George W. Bush and Rudolph Giuliani, the two most compelling Republicans in the country.

John McCain? Yes, I will come to him.

THE CHARACTER FROM TEXAS

Journal entry:

This afternoon [I wrote this entry in the winter of 1998] I spent an hour with the governor of Texas. In Washington for the annual meeting of the National Governors' Association, he had asked a few old Reagan speechwriters to stop by his hotel suite. He wanted advice on setting up a speechwriting operation in Austin. "The reason is," he said, "I'm thinkin' about runnin' for president."

In the course of the meeting Bush reminded me of three different people. First he reminded me of his father. He had the same small, blue eyes, the same furrow in his forehead when he listened intently, even the same way of puckering his lips and twisting his mouth to one side in thought, a gesture so singular that I would have guessed it could only have been duplicated by cloning. Then as he cracked jokes, made tart comments, and chomped an unlit cigar, he reminded me of his mother, a woman who is sharp, quick, funny, and so intent on enjoying herself that if she were a man she would chomp unlit cigars herself. Last, relating a story he used in his speeches, he reminded me of Reagan. He was in a prison, Bush said, visiting young detainees. One black teen had looked him in the eye and asked, "What do you think of me?" The moment had stayed with him. "What kids like that need," he said, "is to know they're not forgotten." The poignancy with which Bush told the story fails to translate into print, but he was nearly as moving as Reagan himself would have been.

One part his father's son, one part his mother's son, one part Reagan. Not a bad mix for a presidential candidate, I thought afterward. Then a second thought occurred to me. Bush had reminded me of other people almost too readily. Who was he?

If you wanted to make the strongest case against the presidential candidacy of George W. Bush, you'd certainly raise the question of his character. It can seem to lack solidity or heft, permitting voters to read into him whatever they'd like, seeing, for example, his father, or, for that matter, I suppose, their own fathers. In New Hampshire last autumn, according to Kellyanne Fitzpatrick, a majority of voters told pollsters that they believed George W. Bush agreed with them on the issues *and* that they didn't know where he stood on the issues. "People just see in him whatever they want," Kellyanne said. "He's that kind of candidate."

Then there is the life story of George W. Bush. It isn't exactly an epic. Bush coasted through Yale, settling for gentleman's Cs. He proceeded from Yale to Harvard Business School, incubator of business titans, then, returning to Texas, failed to become a business titan, instead founding an oil company that went bust. The deal that finally made Bush's fortune was the 1989 purchase of the Texas Rangers. In return for an investment of just over $600,000, of which he borrowed $500,000, Bush received a stake in the team of 1.8 percent. Under the terms of the contract, Bush received an additional 10 percent of the team for serving as general manager. In 1998, when the team was sold, Bush's share of the proceeds came to nearly $15 million. Two points about these transactions are worth noting. The first is that it appears doubtful Bush would have been cut in if his name had been George W. Humperdinck. The second is that the bulk of the profits came not from baseball but from that other national pastime, real estate. The city of Arlington, Texas, built the Texas Rangers a new stadium, named, a little obviously, The Ballpark in Arlington. It paid for the stadium by adding half a cent to the city sales tax. Then the city agreed to charge the team $5 million a year in rent and maintenance, applying the money to the purchase of the stadium at the end of 12 years for a round $60 million. Since that was the amount the team would already have paid, the city in effect agreed to hand the stadium over for nothing. Now, there was nothing underhanded or shady about the arrangement between the Texas Rangers and the city of Arlington—indeed, the people of Arlington overwhelmingly approved of the arrangement in a 1991 referendum. Yet when the Texas Rangers were sold in 1998, a number of observers believe, the stadium was worth more than the team. The Ballpark in Arlington was the house the taxpayers built, and it made Bush rich.

Even the moment in 1987 when, at the age of forty, Bush quit drinking, turns out to have been less of an accomplishment than it might seem. At dinner with friends one night, he drank too much. The next morning he went for a jog, developed a headache, and decided to give up drinking. Just like that. He never underwent anything remotely akin to the struggle of a genuine alcoholic. All George W. Bush appears to have done instead is drop an adolescent habit a little later in life than most frat boys.

Yet by the time this book appears, the former president of the DKE fraternity at Yale may very well stand only a day or two away from receiving the Republican nomination for president of the United States. As early as the spring of 1999, when I spent a couple of days traveling with him in California, Bush had established himself as the front-runner. His lead over his opponents for the Republican nomination was more than 40 percentage points. He had already raised over $30 million, more than all his opponents for the nomination combined. Bush had acquired the trappings not just of a leading candidate for president but of a president himself. He crisscrossed the state in a Boeing 707. He drove through Los Angeles, Sacramento, San Francisco, and Silicon Valley in motorcades, Bush himself in a limousine, his staff following in sedans, the press at the rear in two big buses, police on motorcycles everywhere. At each of his stops, crowds gathered, hoping to catch a glimpse of him. One reporter, looking out the window of the press bus at Bush, who was signing photographs for a moment before stepping into his limousine, shook his head and muttered, "Just look at it. He's already got everything but the sirens."

A frat boy? Who already had everything but the sirens? Why did Republicans permit this to happen?

Because the frat boy came to their rescue.

After watching both George Bush and Bob Dole go down in defeat to Bill Clinton, after seeing the Republican majority in the House of Representatives shrink over the last five and a half years from 26 to just 11 seats, after observing the rout that the GOP candidates for governor and senator suffered in California in 1998, Republicans had come to think of themselves as Nell, tied to the railroad tracks as the whistle of an approaching train shrieks in the distance. George W. Bush was their Dudley Do-Right, the man who had come to cut the ropes, lift the Republicans onto his steed, and gallop away to safety.

Tick down the list of problems for the Republican Party that we have encountered in this book. George W. Bush solves nearly every one.

The divide between economic and social conservatives? The two sides may loathe each other, but they both fawn over Bush. Economic conservatives see him as practical and down-to-earth. "A lot of us here in the valley have operations in Texas," I heard John Chambers, president and CEO of Cisco Systems, say at a fund-raising event for Bush in Silicon Valley. "We know we can do business with him." Social conservatives believe Bush shares their values. For all the hell-raising Bush may have done as a fraternity president, today he is a born-again Christian, a devout Methodist who makes certain to turn up in church every Sunday.

The danger that the GOP has become too southern? That

it risks alienating everyone who doesn't speak with a drawl? George W. Bush was raised in Texas. Yet he was educated, so to speak, abroad, attending Andover, Yale, and Harvard. When southerners look at him, they see not a Yankee but one of their own. When northerners look at him, they see not a redneck but the product of a New England education.

The GOP's difficulty in attracting African-Americans, Catholics, and single women? Bush has proposals that appeal to each. His education program includes vouchers, which, as we have seen, have the support of African-Americans. His welfare reforms include "faith-based initiatives," programs that, as we have also seen, would transfer some of the functions now performed by government agencies to private organizations, including religious groups, an instance of compassionate conservatism that Catholics and single women find reassuring.

The need to win over Hispanics? Hispanics, polls indicate, take to Bush as to no other presidential candidate. For his part Bush has wooed them as he has no other group. He delivered portions of both his inaugural addresses as governor in Spanish. He has appointed Hispanics to high positions in his administration. When he visits their neighborhoods, Bush appears so much at ease with Hispanics that they might as well be members of his family (which, for that matter, some are—Bush has Hispanic nephews and a Hispanic niece, the children of his brother Jeb, who is married to a Mexican). Hispanics respond by returning the compliment, treating Bush like one of their own.

Now consider Bush's electoral advantages. He already commands the support of Texas, the second-most populous state in the nation. His brother, Jeb, is governor of Florida, giving Bush an edge in the fourth-most populous state. And given

Bush's appeal among Hispanics, he stands a good chance of carrying California, the most populous state. What Republicans therefore see in George W. Bush is something they haven't had in a long time now—when my research assistant, a sophomore at Stanford, mentioned that he was just seven the last time a Republican captured the White House, I realized just how long: a presidential candidate who can win.

Yet the question that I asked myself after meeting Bush lingers in many Republican minds all the same. Why isn't his character more sharply defined? Why doesn't it have more heft? I myself found that the question of Bush's character troubled me most when I compared him with a man who, like him, was born into privilege and then, like him, devoted himself to public service. The person I had in mind was his father.

By the time President Bush was as old as Governor Bush, he had served as a pilot in the Second World War, helped to build up the Republican Party in a Texas that was still solidly Democratic, and played a leading role in the decisive struggle of the second half of the twentieth century, the Cold War, confronting the Soviets as our ambassador at the United Nations. Compared with his father, it seemed to me, George W. Bush looked slight.

Then I had a disconcerting thought. Precisely the same could be said about me when compared with my own father. By the time he was my age, my father had worked his way through the Great Depression by digging ditches with a road crew, the only job he could find once he left high school, spent more than four years at sea during the Second World War, then returned home to marry and, without ever having had the chance to go to college, enter the workforce to support his family.

My point, of course, is that our parents and we—by "we"

I mean my fellow baby boomers and I—had two entirely different sets of formative experiences. Our parents overcame the Depression, defeated Hitler, rebuilt the American economy, and sustained a long and finally successful struggle against the Soviet Union. Tom Brokaw's book about our parents, *The Greatest Generation*, spent weeks on the best-seller list because it captured the truth. The events that shaped our parents made them into giants. We came of age during a long run of peace and prosperity. Our parents wanted it this way. They worked long and hard to give us just the world in which we grew up. The United States was secure. It provided a rapidly rising standard of living for its citizens. Peace and material well-being were, so to speak, our inheritance. But now we face the same question that always faces kids who inherit a lot. How can we live up to our old men?

The valid comparison isn't between George W. Bush and his father. It's between George W. Bush and members of our own generation. Compare Bush with me, and he looks good enough to have his face carved on Mount Rushmore. Compare Bush with his opponents for the Republican presidential nomination and, I would contend, he still looks pretty good.

Steve Forbes? I admire the boldness with which Forbes articulated an explicitly conservative agenda. But suggesting that voters send him directly from *Forbes,* a magazine that he and his brothers inherited, to the Oval Office? You could call that audacity. You could also call it lousy judgment. Steve Forbes should have run for the senate from New Jersey. I hope he still does. Gary Bauer? Alan Keyes? Both contributed to the campaign by raising the level of debate. But if either ever thought the voters should actually make him president, he was guilty of the same lousy judgment as Steve Forbes.

Now I come to John McCain.

McCain's five and a half years as a prisoner of war in Hanoi set him apart from other baby boomers, needless to say. But while McCain seldom fails to display his remarkable past—photographs of McCain in his flying gear are often in evidence when he speaks, and McCain himself drops references to his years as a POW throughout his remarks—he is always a little vague when he describes the future. On foreign policy, he sounds emphatic enough, but his views lack any overall coherence. He announced his tax plan weeks after Bush made public his own plan, and an economist friend who has studied the McCain offering tells me that the numbers still don't quite add up. Of course there is a reason for this. McCain pays little attention to policy because he understands that it is peripheral to his campaign. The man of character is running on character alone.

One McCain supporter I know granted every charge against McCain that I made. The tobacco deal that McCain supported in the Senate amounted to little better than a gigantic tax hike on smokers, mostly people of modest means. His campaign finance proposal is flatly unconstitutional. His tax plan would cut taxes by even less than the amount President Clinton proposed in his last state of the union address.

"Look, my issue profile fits a lot better with George W. Bush," the McCain supporter said, "and I'm totally against McCain on his tax plan. But the issues threshold is lower these days. We're not running in 1980. History no longer hangs in the balance. What the American people want after eight years of Bill Clinton is to take a shower."

By "take a shower," he of course meant repudiate Bill Clinton by defeating Al Gore. Fine and good. Lord knows I'd like to see Republicans do just that. But defeating Al Gore would require just one day, election day. Afterward, McCain would have almost three months to fill before taking his oath of office, then four years to get through before his term as president ended. Is it too much to ask how he would pass the time? What I see when I look at McCain, in short, is a curious paradox. By running on character alone, McCain is demonstrating a lack of character itself.

By contrast, George W. Bush has assembled a national campaign organization, an undertaking that none of his opponents, including McCain, who at this writing is still putting his state organizations together on the fly, ever even attempted. He has gathered knowledgeable advisers on every aspect of national policy. He has announced a tax plan that goes to the trouble of making certain the numbers all add up, an intricate exercise that, as I've said, McCain still hasn't bothered to get right. He has detailed a foreign policy that amounts to the most impressive statement of American ends, and of the means we will need to accomplish those ends, put forward by any politician since the Cold War.

Bush's positions lie squarely within the Republican tradition—and Republicans know it. Add up the Republican vote in the primaries that have taken place as of this writing— New Hampshire, Delaware, South Carolina, Michigan, and Arizona—and you'll find that Bush defeats McCain by six percentage points. Toss in the Independent vote. Bush is still ahead, outpacing McCain by four percentage points. Only when you add the votes cast by Democrats—Democrats, mind you—does McCain come out on top.

Now, if John McCain wins the Republican presidential nomination, you can certainly count on me to support him. Even if McCain made up his policies as he went along, he'd be so much better as president than Al Gore that I wouldn't have any trouble working up real enthusiasm for his cause, plastering my bumper with McCain stickers and putting a McCain button on my lapel. But I expect McCain to lose, not win. Over the next few weeks, it's my guess, Republicans will rally to George W. Bush, the compassionate conservative, despite the insurgency of John McCain, the—well, the whatever it is that McCain is. And if I'm right, Bush will have added a second paradox to this campaign. By standing on the issues, he will have proven his character.

Journal entry:

Like all presidential libraries [I made this entry after attending the dedication of George Bush's presidential library in College Station, Texas, in November 1998], the Bush Library includes a museum that displays various aspects of the president's life. Wandering through the museum yesterday, I decided that the most impressive exhibit was an airplane, suspended from the ceiling, identical to the one in which George Bush was shot down over the Pacific during the Second World War. I happened to notice a couple of old geezers looking up at the plane. They were both wearing what I at first took for baseball hats. Then I saw that the hats bore the inscription, "U.S.S. Finback." The Finback. Of course. That was the submarine that pulled the eighteen-year-old George Bush out of the Pacific after he had spent the night on a raft, bobbing toward an island occupied by the Japanese. Old geezers? Heroes.

Across from the library itself an enormous tent, two or three times the size of a circus tent, had been erected for

*the festivities. Yesterday, the day before the dedication cer-
emonies, the tent was the site of a Texas barbecue—five or
six hundred people, the men in jackets and ties, the women
in suits and, many of them, jewels, seated at big round ta-
bles eating chicken with their fingers. President Bush went
from table to table, greeting every person in the tent.*

*Then today, after the dedication ceremonies themselves,
a second barbecue took place in the tent. The same five or
six hundred people all returned to eat another round of
chicken. But this time President Bush was absent; he and
Mrs. Bush were in the library for a private luncheon with
their guests, Lady Bird Johnson, President and Mrs. Ford, President and Mrs. Carter, Mrs. Reagan, and President and Mrs.
Clinton. The figure who stood in for President Bush, circulating from table to table shaking hands, was Governor Bush.*

*Watching George W. Bush, it occurred to me that the
political infrastructure that it had taken his father a life-
time to assemble—the people in the tent included scores of
political operatives and donors—was passing intact from
father to son. Then I began to wonder what the son's presidential library might look like. Where his father's library
had an airplane hanging from the ceiling, would his have
a scale model of the DKE house at Yale?*

*George W. Bush is smart enough to know that he's been
lucky. And now that we're down to members of our generation I can't think of anyone likely to do the job of president as well. If George W. Bush has the guts to go for the
big one, the Republican Party ought to say a prayer of thanks.*

YOU'RE A BIGOTED PERSON, MONROE

Probably the best way to see the mayor of New York City in action is not to see him at all but to hear him. Rudolph Giuliani hosts two live call-in radio shows every week. On a Friday morning in the spring of 1999, I sat in on one of the mayor's broadcasts, WABC's *Live from City Hall*. The setting, the mayor's office in city hall, is a high-ceilinged room with a chandelier, paned windows, tasteful sofas and armchairs, and a thick carpet patterned with a geometric design. It conveys just the impression of sedate and historic tastefulness that many law firms and investment banks spend a great deal of money to attain. I almost expected to see Alexander Hamilton enter the room wearing a frock coat and a powdered wig. Instead Rudy Giuliani walked in in his shirt-sleeves, his thinning hair swept back over his forehead. He nodded quickly to the radio technicians in the room, then sat down at his desk, beneath a portrait of his favorite mayor, Fiorello La Guardia, slipped on a pair of earphones, and tapped the microphone, asking a technician, "You're sure this thing is working, right?" Waiting for airtime, Giuliani glanced over papers on his desk, making notes.

A technician announced that there was one minute to go. Glancing up, Giuliani noticed that I was trying to read the brass plaque on the front of his desk. "The desk was La Guardia's," he said. "Ed Koch used to use it. Then David Dinkins sent it off to Gracie Mansion [the official residence of New York's mayors]. Can you believe that? I brought it back and had it raised. La Guardia was barely over four feet tall. I kept banging my knees."

The technician began the countdown. Three . . . two . . . one.

"Hello, everybody," the mayor began. "This is Rudy Giuliani speaking to you from city hall." He would get to callers in a few moments, Giuliani explained, but first there were a few items he wanted to mention. In the course of the next three minutes he discussed half a dozen topics, staring off into the room as he engaged in a staccato, stream-of-consciousness monologue.

First he was the city historian, explaining the construction taking place around city hall. "We're restoring City Hall Park to its nineteenth-century glory," Giuliani said. When workers started turning up old objects, Giuliani had called in archae-ologists. They had identified everything from minor, everyday items such as old bottles and toothbrushes to sites of major interest, including burial grounds. "The city has a history that goes back to 1625 when the Dutch first settled here. In the very early days, the character of the city was set, and the char-acter of the city remains the same today. It's a business city. The area of Wall Street was used for trading items way back as early as 1634 or 1635. Teachers, if you're looking for a good field trip for your class, we'll have a big historical dis-play here in city hall when the construction is completed."

Next Giuliani became the city's top basketball fan. "Talk-ing about the present, tonight the Knicks take on the San An-tonio Spurs, and they're down three games to one." The mayor told his listeners not to worry. The Knicks would end the se-ries by winning the next three games. "It's exactly where the Knicks *want* to be, with their backs against the wall. In an underdog team, it's the only way in which they can really function." (The Knicks lost that night, ending the series.)

Next Giuliani became in effect the secretary of defense. Moving from a basketball team to the defense establishment of the entire nation, he conveyed no awareness that he had jumped from a small topic to a big one. He simply kept talking.

In a recent speech, Giuliani explained, he had mentioned that the Clinton administration had permitted the nation's defense spending to fall to historic lows. "You know what? Somebody in the Clinton administration said my figures were wrong. So I went and checked. I was absolutely right." Reading from a memo that a member of his staff had prepared— the only time throughout the broadcast that Giuliani referred to notes—he reeled off a string of figures. "Defense spending as a proportion of GDP," he concluded, "has dropped to the lowest level since the Great Depression back in the 1930s, during the time that we were disarming after the First World War without anticipating the Second World War. So like I said, I was absolutely right."

Then Giuliani became the city's head nurse, urging New Yorkers to donate blood to the Red Cross, which was facing a shortage of Type O supplies. He wasn't offering a pleasant suggestion. He was barking out a civic duty. "Everybody who's eligible should donate *now*." He had just donated blood to the Red Cross himself. "It doesn't hurt—well, except for a little prick. It's good for your character development, anyway."

Next Giuliani took on the role of a priest, offering inspiration. He told the story of a young girl, Jamie, who was fighting a brave battle against cancer. He had been keeping his listeners posted on Jamie. "So I just wanted you to know that she graduated from fifth grade at P.S. 91 yesterday and she's doing just fine. She inspires all of us about how to face life and make the most of it."

The mayor tapped a pencil on his desk. Moving to the last topic before taking calls, he became New York's social director. "And now to another point, the Gay and Lesbian Pride Parade on Sunday. It's going to be a terrific parade—a great opportunity for New York to show how we are the most tolerant, the most loving, the most understanding city, in which people of different views about politics, religion, and sexual orientation can see our connection as human beings."

City Hall Park, the New York Knicks, the national defense budget, a Red Cross blood drive, a little girl fighting cancer, and the Gay and Lesbian Pride Parade. At first I couldn't see anything uniting these disparate topics except the mayor's intense nervous energy. Then I got it. Listening to Giuliani was like taking a walk down Broadway. You'd see office towers, theaters, diners, rich people, poor people, whites, blacks, Jews, and Hispanics, and all that united them would be the buzz and energy of the city. Rudy and the city, the city and Rudy. Say what you want about him, but he manages a feat that only a bravura politician could accomplish. He personifies New York.

The mayor handled the first three calls without incident. Rocco from Brooklyn, a guard in a public school, called in to complain that his superiors had transferred him to guard duty in the prison on Rikers Island. Giuliani spent a few puzzled moments trying to figure out what had happened—a school guard should never have been transferred to prison duty—then told Rocco to stay on the line while he had somebody in one of the deputy mayor's offices talk to him. "T'anks, Mayor," Rocco said. "I t'ink you're terrific."

Anna from Harlem complained about garbage collection. Judith from Queens complained about bus service. Giuliani had them, too, stay on the line to speak to people in a deputy mayor's office, but not before demonstrating a detailed knowledge of the routes of the city's garbage trucks and buses. Anna and Judith both proved effusive in their thanks. Giuliani beamed and thanked them in return.

Then came the call from Monroe in Staten Island.

Monroe informed Giuliani that the Republican leader of the Senate, Trent Lott of Mississippi, had once spoken before a white supremacist group. Monroe asked whether the Republican mayor of New York approved of Lott or would be willing to denounce him over the air. As Monroe spoke, Giuliani's smile disappeared. His forehead creased in concern. He glanced across the room at his press secretary, Sunny Mindel raising his eyebrows as if to ask whether she was aware of the charge against Senator Lott. Mindel shrugged. "I don't know anything about it," she mouthed. Giuliani shrugged back. Then he attacked.

"I get the sense that this is a set-up question," Giuliani said. "I'll tell you what, Monroe. What do you think Democrats should do about Al Sharpton?" Monroe began to accuse Giuliani of changing the subject, which Giuliani had certainly done. Giuliani cut him off.

"Monroe, Monroe, Monroe, Monroe, you are a prejudiced, bigoted person. I have nothing to do with racists of any kind. I have nothing to do with people who cause fires using the fuel of anti-Semitism [Al Sharpton once called a Jewish merchant in Harlem a "white interloper"; later, the merchant's store was torched]. The mere fact that you don't want to deal with it [the question about Al Sharpton] tells me you don't want to be fair and impartial. The Republican Party has a problem with some people wanting to be involved with it who appeal to racism. The Democratic Party has people like that in it also. You've got to be willing to stand up against both of them. I want nothing to do with racism, and I can be clear and unambiguous about it whether it's Republicans or Democrats. But I think you are unable to do that, Monroe. I think you use racism as a partisan tool. Now we'll take a short break and be right back."

Monroe had asked Giuliani a legitimate question. Not only refusing to provide an answer, Giuliani had denounced Monroe for even asking. If Monroe in Staten Island hung up infuriated, he would not have been the first New Yorker to feel that way after an encounter with the mayor.

Born to a working-class Italian family in Brooklyn in 1944, Rudolph Giuliani attended Bishop Loughlin Memorial High School, then got a bachelor's degree from Manhattan College and a law degree from New York University. At the age of twenty-six, he joined the office of the United States Attorney for the Southern District of New York, and, three years later, he found himself assigned to the narcotics unit, where it was his job to go after some of the most despicable people in New York, drug dealers. Less than a decade later, at the age of thirty-nine, Giuliani was himself appointed United States Attorney for the Southern District of New York. In his seven years in the position, he won 4,152 convictions, sending to prison still more despicable people—murderers, mafiosi, white-collar criminals—while suffering only twenty-five reversals. Giuliani's experience as a prosecutor taught him to see life simply, as a battle between the forces of good and evil. If he sometimes overreacts, treating ordinary citizens as suspects, as he did Monroe, New Yorkers appear willing to indulge him. They recognize that by 1993, when Giuliani was elected, the city needed an avenger. The mayor's temper, his high-handedness, his penchant for going on the attack—all have earned him a dedicated corps of critics. Yet to many New Yorkers, these very traits prove that he is the right man for the job.

Since taking office Giuliani has cut the crime rate in half, the murder rate by 70 percent. True, the crime rate has fallen in other cities during the same period. But it has fallen further in New York, making the city, according to FBI statistics, the safest city of more than one million inhabitants in the country.[*] Giuliani has enacted more than $2.3 billion in tax reductions, cutting the personal income tax, the commercial rent tax, the hotel occupancy tax, and the sales tax on clothing. Giuliani has reduced New York City's welfare rolls by half a million, a number so big that if all the people the mayor has moved off welfare established a city of their own, it would be the twenty-seventh biggest in the nation. Since Giuliani took office New York City has created 325,000 new jobs and seen its unemployment rate drop by almost half. If tangible accomplishments represent the measure of a politician, then Giuliani may be the most effective politician in the nation. Yet Giuliani himself is proudest of something that cannot be seen or quantified. It is the new way New Yorkers think about their city.

"New Yorkers used to assume several things about the city," Giuliani said after the radio show. He slouched in an armchair across from his desk, his legs stretched out, his arms behind his head. "They assumed that it had to be dangerous, that it had to be dirty, that we were a welfare capital and we would stay that way, and that the city was unmanageable. That thinking is gone now."

Raised a Democrat, Giuliani explained, he became a Republican for three reasons. The first was the expansion of the welfare state. "I recognized that the alignment of the parties was changing during the 1970s, and I did not agree with the dependency philosophy that the Democratic Party was embrac-

---

[*]Giuliani has only managed to bring down the crime rate, his opponents often charge, by using police brutality. The charge fails to withstand scrutiny. In 1999, for example, New York City experienced only eleven fatal shootings, the lowest incidence since the city began keeping records.

ing, particularly in New York City. It seemed to me that the whole concept of entitlement was very, very, very destructive."

The second reason was foreign policy. "I thought that the Democratic Party, at least as represented by George McGovern and his kind of thinking, did not have an appropriate appreciation of how strong America has to be to preserve freedom and democracy," Giuliani said. "The idea that we should demilitarize, that we should underfund the military— they just didn't recognize how dangerous the world is.

"The other thing I started to feel," Giuliani said, explaining his third reason for joining the GOP, "was that the lack of political competition was killing cities. I could see that this decrepit Democratic Party, which was all that existed in cities, was able to count on everybody's votes and not have to do anything for voters in return."

In 1976, Giuliani voted for Gerald Ford, the first vote he had ever cast for a Republican. He has been a Republican ever since.

Giuliani makes many members of his own party uneasy, the more so now that he is running for the Senate. Some, particularly those close to New York's Republican governor, George Pataki, cannot forget 1994, when Pataki was running for governor against the Democratic incumbent, Mario Cuomo. Giuliani crossed party lines to endorse Cuomo. (Asked about it now, all Giuliani will do is shrug and say, "I made a mistake.") Other Republicans object to Giuliani because he is pro-choice, pro–gun control, and, as his radio paean to the Gay and Lesbian Pride Parade made clear, pro–gay rights. They would vote against him if they could. But they can't. In New York politics, Giuliani is as conservative a candidate as they're likely to get.

In any event fixating upon Giuliani's liberal social positions misses a larger point. His central principles are inherently conservative. Limited government. Public order. Individual responsibility. He has demonstrated that acting upon these principles can transform even New York. In so doing, Giuliani has rendered Republicans a larger service than most of them realize. I didn't realize it myself until I wandered the streets of downtown Manhattan, looking for squeegee men.

Journal entry:

When I lived in New York City in 1990, everyone I knew believed that New York, already dirty and dangerous, was bound to get even worse, slowly decaying. The United States might defeat Communism—the Berlin Wall had fallen just a year before—but cleaning up New York would prove beyond our ken.

Everyone had his favorite complaint. The garbage that piled up on street corners when the sanitation department failed to collect it. The countless porn shops clustered around Times Square. The drugs and violence in the city's schools (a joke in my neighborhood: What's the dress code at Julia Richman High? Skirts for the girls, handcuffs for the boys). My own favorite complaint was the squeegee men.

The squeegee men operated an extortion racket. When you stopped your car at a light, they scrawled some soap on your windshield, squirted some water over the soap, then scraped your windshield with a squeegee, often making it dirtier, not cleaner. Either you rolled down your window to pay them a couple of bucks or they snapped off one of your wipers. In one sense, the squeegee men represented nothing but a petty annoyance—what was a couple of bucks from time to time? Yet in another, they proved profoundly disturbing, demonstrating that the city was lawless. If the NYPD couldn't control a few punks in the street, what could it control?

After interviewing the mayor this morning, I took the subway to the Canal Street stop, got out, and walked the streets near the Holland Tunnel, a favorite spot for the squeegee men, who would move among the cars that were backed up at the entrance. I knew the squeegee men were gone—I'd read that much. I still wanted to see it for myself. I walked for twenty minutes. There wasn't a squeegee man in sight.

I may have been overreacting, I grant you. But I felt the same elation I felt the day the Berlin Wall came down. Something good had happened that only a few years before would have been unthinkable.

Different as they are, George W. Bush and Rudolph Giuliani each solves a problem for the Republican Party. As we have seen, George W. Bush demonstrates how the GOP can win. If he can ward off John McCain, Bush stands at least a chance of carrying the voters inside the Finkelstein Box while appealing to those outside it.

Rudolph Giuliani solves a problem that is even worse. Ever since Ronald Reagan succeeded in achieving so much of his agenda, the GOP has suffered from a certain aimlessness—the very aimlessness that I commented on when I began this journey on, so to speak, Mount Reagan. The Berlin Wall is down. Free markets and democracy have swept the world. Our economy is booming. What is left for Republicans to do? But if Giuliani can cut crime in New York, Republicans can cut crime anywhere in the nation. If he can restore a sense of order and pride to New York, Republicans can restore order and pride to any city or town. You see my point. Giuliani has made the unthinkable thinkable. If millions of American children are trapped in mediocre public schools, why shouldn't Republicans enact voucher programs to get them out? If the federal government still spends an amount equal to a full one fifth of the GDP, why shouldn't Republicans scale the federal government back? Or reform the tax code? Or privatize Social Security? Giuliani himself might dissent from a social agenda, but why shouldn't Republicans reduce abortions? Or strengthen the institution of marriage?

To my mind, Rudolph Giuliani and the revival of New York do indeed rank right up there with Ronald Reagan and the fall of the Berlin Wall. Giuliani, like Reagan, has shown Republicans that their principles are more powerful than even they themselves often suppose.

As I was about to leave his office, Mayor Giuliani said there was something he wanted me to see. He stood, walked to his desk, riffled among some papers for a moment, then found what he wanted and picked it up. He showed me a bound report. "This is hilarious," Giuliani said. "You'll love it."

The federal government, he explained, had just conducted a study of Yankee Stadium, checking it for accessibility to the disabled. The inspectors had found some three thousand instances in which Yankee Stadium failed to meet federal standards.

"Listen to this stuff," Giuliani said. He read one item after another. The path of travel out of the Yankee dugout was accessible only by steps, not a ramp, making it impossible to get a wheelchair onto the field. The dressing bench in the Yankee locker room was forty-five inches long by sixteen inches deep instead of the required forty-eight inches long by twenty-four inches deep. The toilets in the locker room had a seat height of sixteen inches, one inch below the required seventeen inches. The spout of the drinking fountain in the weight room was forty-two inches off the floor instead of the required thirty-six inches.

On and on Giuliani read, howling with laughter. The federal bureaucrats had failed to see that although many duties can indeed be performed by disabled people, including, as Franklin Roosevelt demonstrated, the duties of president, some duties lie outside the grasp of the disabled by their very nature, including the duties of the New York Yankees.

"The urinals are too high," Giuliani continued, cackling. "The toilet paper dispenser is incorrectly mounted on the back wall of the toilet. Do you believe anybody does this? I mean, people get paid to do this."

Giuliani tossed the report back onto his desk.

"The federal government sent people here from Washington to do this. This is the stupidity they use. They are pointy-headed stupid morons. This is ridiculous! This is ridiculous!"

Trying to imagine my fellow Republican, Rudolph Giuliani, as a member of the Senate, I made my way down the marble steps of city hall, then past the men and equipment engaged in restoring City Hall Park. As I stepped back onto the street, I was still smiling.

Epilogue

LOVE?

Journal entry:

By now I've traveled to New York City, Jersey City, Washington, D.C., Seattle, Phoenix, Los Angeles, Fresno, and elsewhere. What strikes me as odd is that so many people I'd never met—people who had no good reason to invite me into their offices—have been perfectly happy to talk to me. All I had to say was that I was writing a book about the Republican Party. They responded with the kind of warmth you might accord to a fraternity brother.

Why? It's not as if belonging to the Republican Party created all that intimate a bond among us. The GOP counts tens of millions of Americans as members.* It administers no entrance examination or membership oath, instead accepting everyone who wants to join. Unlike political parties in Europe, the GOP requires no dues. (Various branches of the GOP—the Republican National Committee, the National Republican Congressional Committee, state party organizations, and so on—will send you junk mail, asking for con-

---

*Strickly speaking, the GOP never counts its members. It can't. There are roughly 29 million registered Republicans, but they all live in the twenty-eight states that permit citizens to name a party when they fill out the paperwork that entitles them to vote. That leaves an indeterminate number of Republicans living in the other twenty-two states. Surveys suggest that among Americans who are old enough to vote, about 30 percent consider themselves members of the GOP, a statistic that would place the number of Republicans at some 61 million. But who knows?

tributions, but you remain equally Republican whether you toss the solicitations in the wastebasket, as I do, or respond to each by writing a check.) Nor does the GOP impose any discipline upon its members. In London recently, a prominent member of the Conservative Party, Lord Archer, admitted perjuring himself in a court of law. The Conservative Party is submitting Lord Archer to an ethics investigation. Depending upon the findings of the investigation, it might expel him. A Republican could admit the same crime—and there would be nothing the GOP could do. Investigate a member? Expel him? The GOP has no mechanism for doing either.

The GOP doesn't even have any authoritative way of articulating its positions. Every four years, it is true, a committee convenes to write the Republican platform. In a European political party, such a platform, or manifesto, as it is often called, would be considered a definitive statement of principles and aims, binding on the party's officeholders and candidates. But if you want to know how seriously Republicans take the GOP platform, just look at Bob Dole. When he ran for president in 1996, the platform included several planks that Dole disliked. Dole dealt with the platform by ignoring it. "The platform?" he would huff whenever a reporter started to ask him about a controversial plank. "Never read it."

Huge, open to anyone, amorphous, utterly undisciplined. Why would anyone even want to belong to such an organization? Yet people spoke to me for one reason. The GOP mattered to them.

I set out on this journey to discover what the Republican Party stands for now that Ronald Reagan is gone. But the journey took on a life of its own, teaching me lessons I hadn't expected. One was that the very way I had approached the GOP, expecting to be able to capture it by coming up with a list of positions, was mistaken. I had the wrong scope or scale in mind. The Grand Old Party proved bigger and older—grander—than I had thought.

Of course the GOP takes positions on the issues. But it has a prior stand, an overarching position that it has held throughout its existence. As one of the two major parties, the GOP helps to keep American politics both stable and vital. In power, it unites disparate elements behind its agenda. Out of power, it serves as a stout critic of the Democratic Party while providing a base from which politicians eager to defeat the Democrats can develop new programs. With a membership made up of particular ethnic, religious, regional, and socioeconomic groups, it has an almost tribal character, giving tens of millions of Americans a sense of personal involvement—a stake—in politics. It is one thing to watch as a disinterested observer while politicians win or lose this or that election. It is another to believe that their victories and defeats reflect upon your own tribe.

A source of stability. A base from which to put forward new programs. A link between ordinary Americans and the political process. Many Republicans don't realize this themselves—I certainly didn't—but before it stands for anything else, the Republican Party stands for the success of American democracy.

To repeat the question I asked at the outset, Who *are* these people? What does George W. Bush have in common with

Rudolph Giuliani, Haley Barbour with David Brady, Michael Medved with Jane Dee Hull, Justin Adams with Newt Gingrich? A discernible set of principles? Or now that the Cold War is over—and Ronald Reagan has departed from the scene—does the GOP amount to nothing more than a tribal affiliation intermixed with a scattering of exiles from the other party? Is its only animating principle, like that of the Whig Party before it, enmity toward Democrats?

Nearly every person with whom I spoke was able to articulate his reasons for being a Republican. A belief in individual responsibility. The conviction that any government that absorbs a full one fifth of the goods and services its citizens produce is too big and too intrusive. The desire to see American military might remain unassailable, even in the post–Cold War world. An eagerness to bring market forces to bear on social problems, introducing voucher programs, for example, to improve our schools, or replacing welfare with workfare. From Fresno to Jersey City, I found, Republicans hold in common a clear set of principles. It is true that on the social issues, Republicans are divided. Yet the main body of the party—the GOP that lies inside the Finkelstein Box—is pro-life, opposes special rights for gays, and supports the institution of heterosexual marriage. While the GOP makes room for a wide divergence of opinion on these matters, it is nevertheless accurate to say that the GOP as a whole stands for traditional morality.

Do the GOP's principles make any difference? Pat Buchanan doubts it. Buchanan says he bolted the Republican Party because its agenda had become all but indistinguishable from that of the Democratic Party. In one sense, Buchanan is merely restating a truism of political science, namely that the two major political parties in the United States are much closer together than political parties in Europe, which run from monarchist to Communist. Yet at the same time Buchanan has a more immediate point. Republicans are in less of a revolutionary mood than they were when Ronald Reagan ran for office in 1980. The differences between George W. Bush and John McCain on the one hand and Al Gore on the other are far smaller than were the differences between Ronald Reagan and Jimmy Carter.

"Ever hear of vectors?" David Brady asked when he and I discussed this. "No, you wouldn't have. It's math." Vectors, David explained, are sets of data with both distance and direction—in effect, arrows. "Start two vectors right next to each other on a graph. Then point them in different directions—just slightly different, a degree different, half a degree different, whatever. The further you plot them, the further apart the vectors become. Follow those two suckers out any distance at all and you'll end up in two completely different places."

Likewise our political parties. Even when they appear close together, the differences between them still add up.

George W. Bush and John McCain may both refuse to promise that they will appoint only pro-life judges to the Supreme Court and the federal bench. Yet either would appoint far more pro-life judges than would Al Gore, who has promised to appoint only pro-choice judges. George W. Bush's and John McCain's plans to cut taxes, boost defense spending, and restrain domestic spending may be tepid compared with those of Ronald Reagan—McCain's plans, since they are so ill-formed, particularly so. To use Kellyanne Fitzpatrick's formulation, Bush's and McCain's plans may amount not to a Republican revolution but to Republican ripples. But either George W. Bush or John McCain would cut taxes, boost defense spending, and restrain domestic spending far more than would Al Gore—and if either Bush or McCain had the support of a Congress controlled by his fellow Republicans, he would cut taxes, boost defense spending, and restrain domestic spending even more. At the end of four years, still more at the end of eight, the nation would find itself in a completely different place under a Republican from where it would end up under a Democrat.

This brings me to a point that I have been trying to avoid.

Throughout this book I have worked assiduously to keep my focus on the Republican Party, suppressing my impulses— and I have felt them repeatedly—to attack the Democratic Party. In just a few pages this book will be over, and you would think that I could make it to the end gracefully, containing myself, civil and well-mannered for just a few hundred more words. I can't. The tension is too much. Permit me to rant.

I begin with the leader of the Democratic Party, Bill Clinton. In recent years President Clinton has told us that "the era of big government is over." Yet early in his administration he enacted the biggest tax hike in more than a decade, then proposed a health plan that would effectively have nationalized one seventh of the entire economy. President Clinton speaks constantly about the need for our armed forces to remain strong. Yet during his administration the navy has been reduced from just under six hundred ships to just over three hundred, combat readiness in every branch of the armed services has plummeted, and military spending as a proportion of GDP has fallen, as Mayor Giuliani noted, to its lowest point since before the Second World War. During the 1992 campaign, President Clinton pledged to make abortion rare. Yet on the very day he was first inaugurated he signed five executive orders extending the role of the federal government in funding abortions. Thus despite his talk about bringing it back to the center—about establishing a new, third way—Bill Clinton presides over a Democratic Party that continues to stand for higher taxes, an ever-expanding welfare state, cuts in the military, and the moral values, if they may be called that, of the sexual revolution.

The Democratic Party wasn't always like this, of course. In 1960 the Democratic presidential candidate John Kennedy actually ran to the *right* of the Republican candidate, Richard Nixon, calling for greater military preparedness. Then, as president, Kennedy proposed massive income tax *cuts.** But today? George McGovern may feel right at home in the Democratic Party of Bill Clinton, but John Kennedy would scarcely recognize it. And even though Bill Clinton has only months remaining in office, Al Gore has done nothing to repudiate any of Clinton's positions, limiting himself instead to occasional tongue-clicking about the president's dalliance with Monica Lewinsky. The Democratic Party might pay lip service to free markets and traditional values. It might manage to keep its more radical impulses in check. But under Al Gore the Democratic Party would remain what it has been under Bill Clinton: a party not of the center, but of the left.

There. I feel better now.

It is easy to find the Republican Party absurd. The GOP calls to mind bland WASPs in New England, television evangelists down South, and feckless members of the House of Representatives in Washington, D.C. It is likewise easy to find the Republican Party pigheaded. The GOP has done al-

---

*The tax cuts were enacted after Kennedy's death.

most nothing to appeal to African-Americans or single women, while its efforts to deal with the growing Hispanic population have so far proven perverse. At times I find myself imagining that the GOP represents the past, its members, the last remnants of an America that was once overwhelmingly white and Protestant, now living in the interior of the country as they make, so to speak, their last stand, steadily dwindling as a proportion of the population. Then I snap out of it. The GOP controls both houses of Congress and holds thirty of the fifty governor's mansions. Its candidate for the Senate in New York, Rudolph Giuliani, one of the most intelligent and colorful politicians in the nation, is an Italian Catholic, not a WASP. One of its candidates for president, George W. Bush, won a majority of the Hispanic vote in Texas the last time he ran for governor, and at this writing he has led Al Gore in the polls for months on end. Another of its candidates for president, John McCain, has just romped through the early primaries by demonstrating that even a Republican can win votes from Independents and Democrats. To my mind, McCain has won too many votes from Independents and Democrats and too few from Republicans. But still.

The GOP may yet go into retreat. Lord knows it has experience at losing. But for now it looks as though the GOP's principles of self-reliance, limited government, and respect for the Judeo-Christian moral tradition have invested it with continuing appeal. Whenever the GOP seems old, fusty, and hopelessly WASPy, I remind myself that this fall it might sweep into power, winning the White House and both houses of Congress. It might. It really might.

A love affair? With the Republican Party? Strange to say it, but yes. The GOP has commanded the loyalty of my family for as many generations back as I was able to check. It stands for principles that I myself share. I figure that somehow or other I owe it a little emotional involvement. And the more I think about it, the more I recognize that my relationship with the GOP bears all the marks of an affair. This is a bizarre notion. I admit that. But I can't shake it. You see, sometimes I find myself thinking about the Republican Party in the middle of the day (when I wonder what Ronald Reagan would have made of the struggle between George W. Bush and John McCain). Other times, I find myself feeling so irritated with the GOP that I want to break off our relationship (last year, when the House Republicans enacted their specious tax cut), but somehow I never do. The bad times are bad (the presidential campaign of Bob Dole), but the good times are good (election night in 1994, when I swilled champagne while watching returns come in showing that the GOP had won control of the House of Representatives for the first time in four decades). The GOP has led me on, like an old love, proving more fascinating the better I've gotten to know it, without ever losing its capacity to annoy, gall, infuriate, and exasperate me.

It's my party.

Journal entry:

"I've had the chance to look at your manuscript," one of the young people who works for my publisher told me the other day. "I'm a Democrat and everybody I know is a Democrat, so don't tell anybody I said so. But a lot of what you write about the Republican Party makes sense. I was really surprised. It made me think about becoming a Republican myself. Well, almost."

The GOP, still kicking.

ACKNOWLEDGMENTS

Gallivanting around the country to talk to Republicans is a good way to max out your credit card, and I am grateful to those who permitted me to pursue this folly without starving. I wish to name in particular the John M. Olin Foundation and its president, William E. Simon, and executive director, James Piereson; the Lynde and Harry Bradley Foundation and its president, Michael S. Joyce; the New Citizenship Project and its chairman, William Kristol, executive director, Gary Schmitt, and former director, Kenneth Weinstein; and my friend and guru, Roger Hertog.

Needless to say, I am indebted to everyone who took the time to speak to me about the GOP. Most of them appear in the text. I hope they are content to see that as their reward. But several who do not appear in the text offered me invaluable help as well. These include Clark Judge, Steven Manacek, and Chase Untermeyer, close friends who provided frequent encouragement, which I needed; Richard Wirthlin, who provided polling data and—this is the tricky part—helped me to understand it; William F. Buckley Jr. of *National Review,* Martin Anderson, John Cogan, Jerry Dorfman, John Ferejohn, Morris Fiorina, and Shelby Steele, of the Hoover Institution, Nelson Polsby, of the University of California at Berkeley, and Jeffrey Hart and Charles Stinson, of Dartmouth College, all of whom provided insights born of minds more rigorous than my own; and John McGraw, who merits a special word. Chairman of the California Republican Party, John got me into Republican events, told me the difference between what seemed to be happening and what was actually happening, and explained what each of the factions in the GOP wants. Without the grounding in Republican politics that John gave me in California, I would have been even more baffled than I was when I turned to the rest of the country.

My assistant, Susan Schendel, contributed immeasurably to the project by being two things the author is not, meticulous and serene. Searching for facts, my research assistant, Sam Abrams, proved prodigious, turning the Internet inside out. Barbara Sedonic of the White House Writers Group joined the project in the final weeks, double-checking all my assertions. The editors of the *Atlantic Monthly* permitted me to base the maps in this book on maps that I first came across in the pages of their magazine. I am indebted to them all.

As I have noted elsewhere, my agent, Richard Pine, suggested the idea for this volume. My editor, John Aherne, proved congenial, which is good, and skillful, which is even better. Colin Fox, who also worked on the book, made several superb suggestions. I am grateful to each. As for my publisher, Jamie Raab—well, there really is no way to account for all that Jamie did to bring this book into being. There is also no way to thank her, although it has crossed my mind to walk up Sixth Avenue on my knees.

I reserve a particular expression of gratitude for the director of the Hoover Institution, John Raisian. John took a deep breath when I told him I wanted to write this book. Then he told me to go ahead. He's the best boss I've ever had.

Which brings me to the five people who endured the most while I was composing this volume. To my wife, Edita, and our children, Edita Maria, Pedro, Nicolás, and Andrés, a promise. Next weekend, I'll put up the basketball hoop.